safe as houses?

safe as houses?

the homeowner's guide to property, inheritance and taxation

liz hodgkinson

KOGAN
PAGE

London and Philadelphia

First published in Great Britain and the United States in 2007 by Kogan Page Limited

120 Pentonville Road
London N1 9JN
United Kingdom
www.kogan-page.co.uk

© Liz Hodgkinson, 2007

The right of Liz Hodgkinson to b
asserted by her in accordance wit

ISBN 978 0 7494 5012 0

HAMMERSMITH AND FULHAM LIBRARIES		
013062596		
HJ	/	584103
336.276	√	£11.99
SBL 07		

British Library Cataloguing-in-Publication Data

A CIP record for this book is available from the British Library.

Library of Congress Cataloging-in-Publication Data

Hodgkinson, Liz.
    Safe as houses? : the homeowner's guide to property, inheritance and taxation / Liz Hodgkinson.
        p. cm.
    Includes index.
    ISBN-13: 978-0-7494-5012-0
    ISBN-10: 0-7494-5012-6
    1. Older people--Housing. 2. Home ownership. 3. Homeowners--Taxation. I. Title.
    HD7287.9.H63 2007
    333.33'808460973--dc22

                                                                    2007026014

Typeset by Saxon Graphics Ltd, Derby
Printed and bound in Great Britain by Cambrian Printers Ltd, Aberystwyth, Wales

Wills:

"It's the most important document anyone ever writes, but it's probably the most common one to be put off until later".

About 70% of the adult population do not have a Will quite simply because they feel that –

- **It's too complicated** – *only if you make it so.*
- **It's too expensive** – *Wills can be made for as little as £40 or less.*
- **I don't want to think about it** – *The State may distribute your assets.*
- **I don't have the time** – *a Will Writer can visit you by appointment.*

Without a Will you die intestate creating a situation where you leave your spouse, civil partner or children to clean up the mess. Worse still if the value of your estate is above a certain financial level your spouse or civil partner may not receive everything. In fact some of your assets could go to people you may not want to receive.

By making a Will you can ensure that –

- You choose who your Executors and Trustees will be to look after your wishes and wind up your estate. They will also hold funds set in trust for beneficiaries until they reach the age at which you wish them to receive.
- Your spouse or partner and children receive as you would wish.
- The age children will inherit at can be stipulated – without a Will they gain full access, perhaps to a large amount at age 18.
- Friends or charities you may wish to leave a gift to can be named.
- A Guardianship clause should be added to your Will to protect minor children. (Under 16 years in Scotland and 18 years in England) The chosen Guardian(s) will then be able to raise the children as you would wish.
- Your funeral wishes can be noted.
- What if one parent dies and the surviving spouse then re-marries. Your Will can be structured to allow your spouse whilst still alive, take benefit from your estate and the children then get the capital on his or her death, not the new partner.

www.willpeople.co.uk

Wills and Inheritance Tax:

On death, no Inheritance tax is payable on the first £300,000 of an individual's estate (2007-08). This sum is referred to as the Nil Rate Band. Inheritance Tax is then charged at 40% on the balance over this threshold. However, all transfers between a husband and wife and civil partners are exempt for Inheritance Tax and therefore no Inheritance Tax is payable on the death of the first spouse. To ensure that maximum benefit is taken each spouse or partners Nil Rate Band is used.

When making your Will you need to consider writing it to redirect an amount up to or equal to your Nil Rate Band into trust to children or another person or persons other than the spouse. This then uses both Nil Rate Bands.

A straightforward Will giving everything to your spouse does not pay any Inheritance Tax. You could even have gifted away up to £300,000 (e.g. to children) without Inheritance Tax being payable and given the rest to your spouse. However by doing so you could leave your spouse in a difficult financial position.

Some benefits of Discretionary Trust schemes are:

- Proper planning can allow an IHT liability to be wiped out or at worst be reduced and yet allow full access and control of assets to the survivor.
- Tax saving up to £120,000 can be made (2007-08).
- Interest free loans can be made to the survivor, repayable on his or her death, reducing their IHT liability further.
- Ensures assets held in trust are not assessed as capital of the survivor should he or she require long term care.
- Guarantees that the trust assets pass to your children rather than say your spouse or partners new partner should he or she remarry.
- The earlier that you take advice the more options you have.

www.willpeople.co.uk

Wills and Long Term Care Fees:

About 70,000 homes are sold each year to pay for long term care and with care costs in excess of £20,000 per annum the value of your property could soon be wiped out. Should you reach a time in your life when you require long-term care provision, the local authority could force the sale of your home to fund your care. This may wipe out all of your assets leaving nothing to pass on to children.

In most circumstances a Property Protection Trust clause in your Will can prevent this by safeguarding the first partner's share of the home.

If the other partner then requires long-term care the local authority will only assess that person's assets as being half the value of the property. The other half, protected in trust, can then be passed on to your beneficiaries.

Take steps to protect your home from the Community Care Act 1990 and have your Will structured to protect the deceased's share being assessed as capital of the survivor.

Some points to be aware of:

- The local authority assess a claimant's ability to pay for care.
- Married couples are assessed individually.
- If the individual has insufficient income the local authority will look to capital assets which include not only savings but the family home.
- The home will be included unless a spouse, relative over 60, disabled person or a child under 16 lives in the property.
- The home is disregarded for the first 12 weeks of care.
- Many people are tempted to give the home away, say to children and continue to live in the property. This is ineffective for Inheritance Tax and can have Capital Gains Tax implications and is unlikely to protect against care fees as the gift to children will be seen as deliberate deprivation so the value of the property will still be seen as capital. There could also be issues should children die, divorce or become bankrupt.

www.willpeople.co.uk

Contents

Acknowledgements

For expert help in preparing this book, the author would particularly like to thank the following excellent organizations: Help the Aged, Age Concern, the Alzheimer's Society, the Association of Retirement Housing Managers and Solicitors for the Elderly.

Financial and taxation expert Paul Ffitch of Sayers Butterworth and my own accountant, Stuart Heenan, were extremely helpful in guiding me through the thorny issues of inheritance tax, now affecting ever more ordinary people.

I would also like to thank leasehold expert Kat Callo, of Rosetta Consulting, for information on enfranchisement for retirement homes.

Many housing issues affecting older people are far from clear or easy to understand, and I was fortunate indeed to be able to call on so many leading organizations and campaigners who are putting so much time and effort into addressing the often very difficult matters raised in this book.

Introduction

Over 70 per cent of British people now own their own homes. This figure goes up to 85 per cent for the over-50s and means that large sections of the populace now have very considerable financial assets indeed.

For very many older people, the value of their home will far exceed anything they might have been able to save up in a pension scheme, especially as the average price of a house in the UK is now £200,000. In fact, for most people coming up to or at retirement, at least two-thirds of their total assets are in property. And according to the Bank of England, the vast majority of 55- to 64-year-olds are sitting on an absolute fortune, as house prices have risen 205 per cent since 1997. They are, without doubt, the richest generation in history.

Previously, older people had little option but to remain in the rented homes where they had probably lived all their lives. But now, the very attractive financial asset that is your home can give you a dazzling array of choices as to how you live your later years. And with any luck, this same property should also yield a nice little legacy for your heirs when you go. So, if you are looking to make the best use of your property for the days when you are no longer earning, what should you do?

You can of course choose to stay put in the house where you may have lived happily for many years, put down very long roots and brought up your family. If the house has fond memories, you may be extremely reluctant to up sticks and move to somewhere smaller. And if you feel you may not be able to afford to stay there on a retirement income or pension, you can always take out an equity release scheme to 'unlock some of the cash in your home', as the advertisements have it. Or there are schemes available that enable you to sell your house and then rent it back, so that you can continue to live in it. In very many ways, your house can now fund your retirement at the same time as enabling you to carry on living in it.

On the other hand, if the family house has become too big and unwieldy or does not hold such happy memories, you may decide to downsize, buy somewhere smaller and cheaper and release a useful sum of cash to enable you to enjoy your retirement free of financial care. You may also want to help your children, or even your grandchildren, on to the property ladder, and downsizing to a smaller home could be one way of freeing up cash to do this.

Downsizing to a handy lock-up-and-leave flat with no garden to worry about can make a lot of sense if you want to spend months on end travelling after retirement. Flats are more secure than houses, easier to look after and less likely to be burgled when you are away.

If you have fallen in love with a particular country, you may wonder about retiring abroad, an option that is beckoning ever more people who no longer need to work for money. The number of 'silver flighters' is increasing every year as ever more retirees realize that, for the price of a small, dismal flat in the UK, they can have a wonderful villa complete with swimming pool, leisure complex close at hand and guaranteed good weather.

Alternatively, you may ask yourself whether renting instead of buying again might be a clever idea. After all, there is a wonderful array of rented homes available nowadays, all over the world, which simply did not exist in the past. Renting enables you to budget very accurately, and can also mean that you have an enviable lump sum in the bank to finance holidays, cruises, grandchildren's school fees or new cars. Renting also means you are free of all the worries of home ownership such as repairs, maintenance and renovation. They are all somebody else's concern when you rent! A growing number of retirees and older people are deciding they no longer want to be bothered with home ownership, and that renting in their later years gives them both money and freedom.

Then, you may be single, married, in a civil partnership, widowed, divorced or excitingly embarking on a new relationship, and all of these factors will influence your choice of housing in later life. No previous generation has ever had so many partnership possibilities as the present 50-somethings.

Finally, there is the ever-increasing array of age-exclusive and retirement housing to consider. At one end of the scale there are the simple age-exclusive developments where you just have to be of a certain age, and where nursing and other care is not provided. Then at the other end of the scale you have complete retirement villages that offer every facility, including 24-hour nursing care, if needed.

Retirement homes come at all levels of the market, from cheap basic units on brownfield sites to highly exclusive and expensive developments with gourmet restaurants, bridge clubs and social events on offer. Several other countries offer retirement homes and villages as well. There are many retirement complexes in Spain, and of course Florida is par excellence the place of the retirement village.

In fact, if you are an older homeowner, it may seem that the only problem is choosing, when there are so many interesting and varied possibilities on offer. This book will help you to make the wisest choice, taking all your circumstances and wishes into consideration.

But nothing comes without a price attached, and overshadowing all of these wonderful potential lifestyle choices in later years is the grim spectre of inheritance tax (IHT), now affecting ever more homeowners as property values inexorably rise.

At one time inheritance tax was levied only on the very rich, but nowadays those who have struggled to buy a modest one-bedroom ex-council flat could find themselves edging dangerously near the limit of this tax. Inheritance tax applies in many countries abroad, as well, so you can't necessarily escape by retiring to another country. In fact, inheritance tax laws in other countries can be even more horrendously complicated and convoluted than in the UK.

All this means that, increasingly, homeowners are having to make property choices – particularly in later life – with inheritance tax in mind. It is a tax that works like no other, as we shall see, and it can seriously reduce the amount of money you were hoping to leave to your heirs. It is very natural to want to leave something to your family and friends. Most people would prefer their children to inherit any wealth they may have accumulated than for it to go to the government. But these days, it is not so easy to cut the government out of your will if your estate is likely to exceed the IHT threshold.

Inheritance tax has become one of the most hated taxes of all time, because of the peculiar way it can operate to turn people out of homes where they may have lived all their lives. In fact, one of the main drivers behind the numbers of same-sex couples registering civil partnerships is to ensure that the remaining partner is *not* turned out of the shared home when the first one dies.

In recent years, the Treasury's civil servants have been working very hard – and very successfully – to remove all remaining inheritance tax dodges. The result is that increasing numbers of ordinary people are tying themselves in knots trying to work out how to avoid paying a tax cleverly designed to clobber you beyond the grave.

Yes, there are all kinds of commercial schemes in existence that offer inheritance tax planning, with the aim of reducing your IHT liability, but they are complicated in themselves and always cost something to set up. If you live long enough after setting up a trust or other inheritance tax planning scheme, you could end up spending more on the avoidance scheme than your estate would pay in tax.

This book explains just how inheritance tax works, so that you can make wise choices with it in mind. There are, it is true, ways in which you can get round IHT to some extent, and these are also described, along with the pros and cons of each choice. But remember that nothing comes scot-free in the inheritance tax world! Every legal tax-dodging device that reduces inheritance tax after your death leaves you that much poorer while you are alive.

But the biggest difficulty with trying to reduce inheritance tax payable on death is, simply, not knowing how long you have got left, or what kind of nursing home or other expensive care you might need in later life. This is something that has certainly not been lost on the Civil Service as they work tirelessly to plug any remaining loopholes in inheritance tax avoidance. It is this factor of not knowing how long you might last that makes financial planning for a wonderful retirement problematic.

You could suddenly drop down dead at 50 or live for another half-century to get your telegram from the Queen. The main way you can escape, or at least reduce, IHT is to give money or assets away while you are still alive and are not expected to die for another seven years. And don't think you can just give everything away years before you are likely to die and forget about inheritance tax. The government have looked into this one, as well, and have devised penalties for trying to dispose of all your assets while still alive.

And then, even if you do give everything away to your children while you are still alive, can you trust them to be as generous with you as you have been with them? The courts are littered with cases of adult children trying to steal money or property from their elderly parents, contesting wills and quarrelling amongst themselves. Some of these cases go on for years and split families irrevocably. Real-life Bleak House stories – where eventually there is no inheritance left – are all too common where money and bequests are concerned.

But IHT and future bequests apart, you need enough money to be able to enjoy the best years of your life, when you are free from work and family concerns, but still have plenty of active, lively years ahead. Inheritance tax is, after all, only paid after you are dead, although it can profoundly affect those still living, as we shall see.

So this book in particular looks closely at all the financial implications of each lifestyle and housing choice you might make. For example, choosing commercial equity release can give you a useful extra lump sum while you are alive, but it severely reduces the value of your estate. Downsizing might seem sensible, but will moving to a smaller place give you enough of a cash reserve to make it worth it? Moving house is, after all, always an expensive business by the time you have paid estate agents, stamp duty, legal fees, moving fees and renovation costs.

If you decide to move to an apartment rather than a house, you will have to pay compulsory service charges, and your property might lose value as the lease runs down. You may need more spare cash to live in an apartment rather than a house, as you will be responsible for your share of maintenance, renovation and upkeep. If there is a lift or a caretaker, for instance, you will have to pay your share of these costs.

Retirement housing is purpose-built for older people but, at the same time, service and maintenance charges can be high, in some cases as much as £3,000 a month. The greater the number of services on offer, the higher the charge. You may have enough money to buy a sheltered home but will you have enough income to carry on living there? It is often said that you may *want* money when you are young, but you *need* it when you are older.

Then would you want to live out your days in a gated community of elderly and extremely elderly people?

And retirement, or sheltered, housing is not so easy to sell as ordinary housing, as it cannot be sold on the open market but only to other qualifying buyers. Then there is usually a transfer premium to pay on the sale, back to the freeholder or management company. This does not apply in the ordinary housing sector.

If you decide to move abroad, your pension and other state benefits might be adversely affected, and in any case you will be in a different tax regime in another country. Will this leave you better, or worse, off than in the home country? And what if you wanted to move back – could you afford it?

If you are thinking about renting rather than buying, would you be happy having less security of tenure than as an owner? Most modern tenancies are based on the assured shorthold tenancy, which operates in six-month chunks, so you could be given just a few months to quit when you imagined you were nicely settled.

Every choice has its pluses and minuses, but even so there will be an option that is exactly right for you, depending on your circumstances, inclinations, state of health and bank balance. The more money you have, the more extensive your choices, of course, but at the same time the more your estate will have to shell out to the government after death.

The government can raid your estate for inheritance tax when you are safely dead, but it can also severely impact on elderly people while they are still alive. If you have assets, including your home, worth more than around £20,000 you will have to pay for at least some of your care when you go into a nursing home. You will be forced to pay for your own care until all your assets have dried up, and you may have to sell your home to fund such care. If the local authority believes you have hidden or sold some assets, it can investigate every single area of your finances, including whether you have already given all your worldly goods away to your children. Then it can demand them back.

So, although you may have financial assets never enjoyed by previous generations, you might have to work hard to protect those assets. If nursing home fees don't wipe out your estate while you are alive, inheritance tax threatens to reduce it severely after you are dead. No wonder today's older people worry constantly about how to hang on to the assets they have worked so hard to acquire, and how best to pass them on to their beneficiaries after death.

Forewarned is forearmed, so while this book describes all the lifestyle options now available to today's older homeowner it also gives up-to-date information on how inheritance tax works. There is a chapter on how care home fees and services operate, and advice on how you can best avoid or minimize giving hard-earned money away to the government.

This book will also be useful for adult children who may have to make difficult decisions on behalf of their elderly parents.

Mostly, today's older homeowners want three major things out of life: to have plenty of money to enjoy all the years that may be left, to have a home that perfectly suits present and future needs, and to have something substantial to leave family and friends. This book will help you to try to achieve all three goals and enjoy to the full the financial freedom that the previous years or decades of hard work have given you.

1   Inheritance tax

It is often said that there is no avoiding death and taxes. But what about when the two come together?

Rarely has a tax been hated so much as inheritance tax, rapidly becoming the main subject of conversation at middle-class dinner parties. This tax, at one time of concern only to the very rich, is now grabbing ever more people's financial assets. At the time of writing, around 4 in 10 homeowners will find themselves – or their estates at least – liable for this tax.

The former Chancellor Roy Jenkins once famously said that inheritance tax was paid only by those who trusted their relatives less than they trusted the Revenue. If this was true once, it is certainly not true now, as this chapter will show.

Ever since the 1970s, ordinary people have been able to accumulate valuable assets, and in most cases their most valuable asset will be their home. Even people who struggled to buy their own council house in the 1980s under Mrs Thatcher's right-to-buy scheme could now find themselves edging dangerously near to the inheritance tax bracket. And as ever more estates are being sucked into inheritance tax, so the government has been devising ever more ingenious methods of plugging any remaining loopholes.

One argument some people put forward in favour of IHT, as it is unaffectionately known, is that it is only levied when somebody dies. As it is a tax payable after death, so the argument goes, the deceased will never know about it, so what does it matter? There is also a school of thought that says that a dead person's money in a sense belongs to nobody ('You can't take it with you'). Nobody will lose except perhaps the disgruntled heirs, who may be rather upset to learn that the Exchequer is, as often happens nowadays, by far the biggest beneficiary.

Nobody willingly leaves their money to the Exchequer, but the Treasury makes sure it gets it anyway, or at least a high proportion. Inheritance tax is payable at a straight 40 per cent of your estate after taking out the nil-rate band. There is no sliding scale or concession, and the tax usually has to be paid before probate is granted. There is simply no getting away with it, as immediately somebody dies his or her executors receive a huge document on which every single financial or saleable asset has to be noted down. Then, if IHT is payable, all of the deceased's accounts are frozen so that no money can trickle out of the estate in the meantime. These accounts are only unfrozen once the tax is paid. Then, and only then, can money and assets be distributed among the beneficiaries.

And to make matters worse, IHT is often referred to as a 'voluntary' tax, with the implication that you don't have to pay it if you don't want to! This is extremely misleading, as I know from bitter experience. Solicitor Caroline Bielanska, of the specialist lawyer group Solicitors for the Elderly, says: 'There are three main ways of reducing or wiping out inheritance tax, and these come down to: spend it or give it away while you are alive, downsize or consider equity release. These all reduce the value of your estate while you are alive, but all may have adverse consequences for your standard of living in the meantime.'

As somebody who recently had to cope with this traumatic, far-from-voluntary and instantly imposed tax, I know that there is far more to it than the government helping itself to a slice of a dead person's estate before it is divided up among the named beneficiaries. The imposition of this tax, and the fact that it is levied on the estates of ever more homeowners as property prices continue to rise beyond inflation, can mean that families are divided for ever, that siblings, partners and children can be left without a roof over their heads, and that well-meaning but often amateur executors face an administrative nightmare that can last several years, even with relatively modest estates.

Here is what Anna Sidwell, writing to the *Guardian* in February 2007, had to say about IHT:

> As it is a tax on something purchased probably years ago, with great emotional value to several people, not just the deceased, it is

both unfair and hurtful. The heirs may have to sell and sever connections to a community they may have learned to love, thus breaking links probably helpful to that community.

Even if you don't give a fig about justice, happiness or community, there is another practical point of economics. Old people may be unable to afford running repairs, and if the heirs know that investing in the property might just take it out of their reach, there is less incentive to help their parents to keep the place smart. The loss is not just to this family, because generally the housing stock in the UK is very old and frail.

Just when there is likely to be a pension gap, it would help if those starting their pension could inherit a house from their circa 90-year old parents. This would reduce the problem enormously for many, and for the government, kill two birds with one stone.

The writer of this letter makes a further point, which is that the very rich most probably can afford to take steps to wrap up their money, put it offshore or into complicated trusts, and avoid this tax. But the ordinary homeowner can't, as it takes a lot of spare assets and very clever tax advisers, in order to do it. So a tax that was originally introduced to cream some assets off the very rich now has the opposite effect of that originally intended, in that it severely reduces ordinary estates and allows the super-rich to get away without paying it.

The sad case of the octogenarian sisters Joyce and Sybil Burden, who have lived together all their lives, illustrates how devastating IHT can be. Their house, worth some £875,000 in 2006, will have to be sold when the first sister dies, in order to pay IHT – and there is absolutely nothing the surviving sister can do about it. This famous test case went right to the European Court of Human Rights, but they still lost. As one sister ruefully remarked: 'If we'd been gay, we would have been all right. But as we are only sisters, one of us will be turned out of our lifetime home.'

The government currently rakes in around £4 billion a year in inheritance tax, a sum that, unlike income tax, is almost laughably simple to collect. The Treasury just demands 40 per cent of whatever value an estate has over the nil-rate band of £300,000 (in 2007, which will rise to £350,000 by 2010).

Inheritance tax, originally levied in 1894 by the then Chancellor of the Exchequer Edward Harcourt, was aimed at reducing the vast country estates of the hugely wealthy landed gentry. In fact, it was to fund what were then known as death duties that the theme parks on huge country estates such as Woburn Abbey and Longleat were originally set up.

Nowadays, though, you do not have to be a Duke of Bedford or Marquess of Bath to be liable for crippling death duties. You just have to be an ordinary person with a home or other assets worth £300,000 or more. And when the average home in the UK is worth £200,000 this means that the majority of homeowners now have homes that come very near the threshold, before savings or any other financial assets are taken into account.

The tax remains controversial and, remarkably, has its adherents. Here is Labour peer David Lipsey, arguing in favour of inheritance tax in the *Guardian* on 12 February 2007:

> You can avoid the tax by gifts *inter vivos*. Schemes are rife that allow couples to take advantage of two £285,000 tax-free allowances and not one. If you have to pay the tax because you inherit a valuable house from your parents, fear not. You are allowed to pay it off over 10 years.
>
> Substantial inheritance is the enemy of equality of opportunity... No one suggests confiscating their wealth while they are living. However, the 'death-trap' brigade wants to protect it from the taxman, even after they have passed on. A group of people less deserving of a tax break it is hard to find.

As against this Peter Girling, of Girlings Retirement Options, who has been working in retirement housing for many years, says:

> In my view, there is no defence of inheritance tax, as it is eroding the capital base of the country. Most ordinary people have struggled to buy property, struggled to pay off their mortgages and the money from their estates would create an opportunity for the next generation, or the one after that, to get on to the housing ladder. But because of inheritance tax, it is becoming increasingly difficult to help your children and grandchildren.

The situation is made worse by the Chancellor's raid on pension funds, which means that, for large numbers of people, their only real capital is their property. Increasingly, people are starting to think that, if the Chancellor is going to steal a large chunk of their estate, they might as well sell up, give the children some money, and get below the IHT threshold, spending as much money as they can afford to in the meantime.

Who is right, Lord Lipsey or Peter Girling? Before making up your mind, read my own IHT diary, compiled after my beloved partner, the writer John Sandilands, died suddenly in 2004. Here was – in modern terms – a relatively modest estate, but its administration caused two years of continuing headache for the executors, who were myself and John's ex-wife, Jo.

When John died suddenly in March 2004, he left a completely up-to-date and clear will and had a nice six-figure sum of money sitting in the bank, no debts or mortgages, and no children to squabble amongst themselves. His estate would therefore have been simplicity itself to administer, but for the spectre of inheritance tax.

Make no mistake, dealing with IHT, which you must do when your grief is at its most raw and intense, is one long nightmare.

15 March, 2004

I go to my evening lecturing job at 6 in the evening. When I return at around 10.30 I get a call to say that John, my beloved partner of the past 12 years, has suddenly died of a massive heart attack while on the phone to a friend. After the phone went dead, the friend drove to his West London flat (we did not live together during the week, but shared a weekend home) and when there was no reply, called the police, who came instantly, and broke the lock to gain entry.

Within those few hours, the police have taken the body to the mortuary and the coroner has been informed. Funeral directors have been contacted. And I knew nothing of it.

16–31 March, 2004

I go to Kingston Coroner's office to identify the body. The Coroner informs the Probate Office and I, as co-executor of his will, receive the inheritance tax forms three days after the death and before his funeral has taken place. My mind turns to blank horror when I flip through the 50 or so pages of the forms. It soon becomes clear that we will have to pay a lot of IHT on the estate. But how? When?

My co-executor Jo Sandilands, John's former wife, and myself, decide to hand the whole thing over to a solicitor. It is just too complicated for us to handle by ourselves. Also, both of us are in too much shock by the sudden and unexpected death to think straight. Plus, neither of us has ever had to do anything like this before, and we have no expertise at all.

The solicitor quotes us £1500 plus VAT to handle probate. I go to the police station to retrieve the keys of John's flat and Jo and I hunt for his will.

All of John's bank accounts are immediately frozen and we can pay no bills, apart from the funeral. Nor can we pay any cheques into the accounts. John rented out two properties; the tenants have their rent cheques returned to them and start to panic about being evicted. We reassure them.

The Probate Department of John's bank expresses trite sympathy for our loss, but refuses to pay any outstanding bills, even though there is nearly £200,000 in the accounts, more than enough, we hope, to pay the IHT. When asked how we settle outstanding bills, we are told curtly to 'get a loan.'

We have to get hold of John's original will, not a copy, and Jo and myself both have to sign for it in person in front of the solicitor. Probate cannot commence without the original will. We also need the birth certificate, and at least a dozen copies of the death certificate, which is issued only after the post-mortem. Copies are demanded by every utility and official body, before they will agree to stop the service.

April 2004

The first job is to get John's assets valued for Probate. This includes cash at the bank, real estate, stocks and shares, vehicles, jewellery, paintings, antiques, furniture. Even Ikea furniture; in fact, anything which may have a saleable value.

The Probate Office will only accept written valuations made by appropriate professionals, so we get estate agents to value John's properties, six in all – three owned by him and three owned jointly by John and myself. Nowadays, estate agents charge for Probate valuations, and it has become a source of revenue for them. Ours agree to waive the charges if we put the properties on the market with them.

None of these properties can be sold until we receive the Grant of Probate which in turn cannot happen until the IHT is paid. It looks as though we will have to pay around £165,000 IHT on the sum total of his assets of around £800,000. The properties that John and myself jointly owned, including our holiday flat, are not exempt from IHT but are included in the calculations.

But – thank goodness John left his half of the joint flats to me in his will; otherwise I would have had to sell them, as well as his own properties.

Jo and myself and another beneficiary pay for the Memorial Event ourselves. Otherwise, caterers, photographers and other small operators could wait for up to a year to be paid.

We cancel telephone, council tax, insurance, AA subscription, etc and inform all utilities and credit card companies of his demise. This takes a surprising amount of work and effort. Every week, though, letters come to his address demanding payment. We get threatening letters from debt collectors; British Gas threatens to break into the flat and turn off the gas supply unless the account – less than £50 – is paid forthwith.

We spend hours on the phone explaining that we cannot pay bills because the accounts are frozen and will remain so until Probate is granted.

April–August 2004
Nothing whatever happens, except that the threatening (and very upsetting) letters continue to arrive. We receive an offer for John's home and explain that we cannot sell it until we receive the Grant of Probate, which is itself dependent on the Inland Revenue accepting the solicitor's estimation of the total value of John's assets. We donate John's car to Jo's teenage son and the solicitor values it at £100.

We learn slowly what we can and cannot set against IHT. Every monetary or saleable asset, however small, is liable to be included. There are certain things, however, that we can set against the final amount, such as all bills, tenants' deposits, outstanding income tax, cost of the Memorial Service and estate agents' fees. Legal fees, however, are not included and must come out of the remainder of the estate. Our solicitor is meticulous, if excruciatingly slow.

August–October 2004

Jo and myself have to go to another solicitors and sign the probate forms after swearing on the Bible in front of an official. This little escapade costs us £18. We receive an offer on another of John's properties. The solicitor tells us that we, the beneficiaries, are liable for Capital Gains Tax on the sales, if the sale price is in excess of the probate valuation. This is to prevent deliberately low probate valuations.

October 2004

Eight months after John's death we are granted Probate after inheritance tax, amounting to £165,000, is paid. Bank accounts are now unfrozen and wound up. Thank goodness, we agree, that John is not alive to know how much of his hard-earned, taxed money went straight to the government.

The sale on John's home falls through at, quite literally, the eleventh hour, just when we were about to exchange. At 10 am I get a call from the estate agent to say they should exchange within the hour. I tell them I must go to John's flat to pick up some remaining items first and when I return at 11 am, I get a call to say the sale has fallen through.

November 2004

There is no more interest in John's home, but one sale goes through, extremely slowly, on a rental flat. Otherwise, the market seems to have gone completely dead.

December 2004

We decide to rent out John's home rather than have it standing empty, and a tenant moves in. As executors, we are, after Probate, allowed to rent out John's property and receive rents. The tenant, however, stays just one day and the flat goes back on the market. We keep the one month's deposit already paid.

January 2005

We receive a lengthy statement of account from the probate solicitor and get all the paperwork back. It is more than a foot high. We are horrified to discover that the solicitor's bill comes to much more than expected: £3,600 plus £800 for the 'abortive sale' of one of the flats. This money is taken out of John's account before the balance is paid to us as executors.

Yes, we should have shopped around, we should have got written estimates but we were simply not thinking straight at the time.

By the time all the bills are paid, including accumulated service charges on the three flats, there is just £1,300 left of the nearly £200,000 in John's account at the time of his death. We have also had to pay income tax which meant filling in another horrific form.

Jo and myself set up a joint bank account with the £1,300 as we can now receive and pay cheques. We can also start to pay the beneficiaries, including ourselves, once we receive the monies from the sale of the flats.

We exchange contracts on one of John's rental flats. Thank goodness at least one has gone; still no interest in the other two.

February 2005

Almost a year has elapsed since John died and we still have not tied up the estate. Two properties remain unsold, and who can say how long they will take to go? At least the beneficiaries have had the first tranche of their money, and the paperwork is no longer piling up so fast although demands for service charges continue. Council tax has to be paid again on unsold and empty properties six months after Probate.

Even when using a solicitor, there is endless work for the executors when IHT has to be paid. There is, we realised, no real way of wriggling out of this tax. The Inland Revenue can – and do – query absolutely everything.

Sept–Oct 2005

We finally manage to sell John's two other flats and pay the six beneficiaries, who receive a total of just over £73,000 each – a nice sum no doubt but for each person, less than half of what the Chancellor has pocketed.

February 2006

Jo and myself have kept £2000 in our joint executors' account, in case of unexpected or unforeseen bills. At long last, it seems to be over, so we divvy up the remainder of around £300 each, and close down the account, 23 months after John died.

Finally, the agony is over, but our sharpest and saddest memory is the huge amount we had to pay to the Exchequer. We will never forget that.

(published in the *Daily Express*, 18 February 2006)

And John had done all the things that IHT experts advise: he had an up-to-date will, plenty of money in the bank, no debts, no mortgages and no outstanding loans. Plus, he had thoughtfully provided Jo and myself each with a comprehensive list of his bank, pension, accountant, solicitor and other such necessary financial details.

The big question is, now that financial consultants are making a lot of money advising people how they can avoid or minimize IHT, could he, or we, have done anything to avoid this payment? The sad answer is: no, not really. John needed his lump sum in the bank, plus the rents from his properties, to live on when he became too ill to work. He could have gradually disposed of his assets up to seven years before he died but, not only did he not know how long he had got, he didn't know how much money he might need to fund his declining years. And although administering his estate was a lot of work for his executors, at least it meant he lived out his last years free of financial worry. And, yes, theoretically he could have paid into an insurance scheme to cover IHT on his death but the premiums – for somebody of his age and poor state of health – would have been too high to be easily affordable.

He did consider giving a flat away to each of his three relatives, but that would have involved them in capital gains tax, plus dealing with assets that could easily turn into liabilities. Before he died – although we were not expecting such a sudden death – we racked our brains to try to find any way out of paying the Chancellor of the Exchequer a large six-figure sum but we could not come up with anything whatsoever that remotely worked. So – this tax is not as 'voluntary' as it is often made out to be.

If he had known for certain exactly when he was going to die, John might have made some very different arrangements. We can all say that, but with few exceptions none of us know how long we have got. And this fact has not been lost on the government or, more accurately, the scores of civil servants whose task is to look at inheritance tax and find ever more ways of circumventing the loopholes.

Not everybody realizes that IHT is payable up front, often before property or other assets can be sold. A letter to the *Daily Mail* on Wednesday, 26 July 2006, says:

> My relative, a widow, died in January. The shares in her estate were then valued. There was not enough money in her bank account to pay IHT on the whole estate so a bank loan had to be arranged. The value of these shares has now decreased. If this is still the case when they are sold, will there be an adjusting refund of IHT to reflect this? I was surprised at having to pay IHT upfront (thus having to incur the cost of the loan) and consider it most unfair.

The *Mail*'s 'money doctor', Margaret Stone, replied that, yes, you can ask the Capital Taxes Office to revise the IHT if the value of the shares has fallen. If the value has gone up, however, the IHT bill would not go up but there could then be a capital gains tax liability instead. Margaret Stone added:

> IHT must be paid within six months. You can pay by instalments but interest will be charged, currently at 3pc. Annual instalments can be spread over ten years but full settlement can be made earlier. Interest has to be paid over that 10 years, of course, making the eventual IHT bill much higher than if it were paid all at once.

I also know from the experience of my ex-husband when sorting out his mother's effects that, if your estate is even anywhere near the threshold, the Revenue will minutely examine all your bank accounts plus those of any beneficiaries or relatives, to make sure no large sums have been transferred with the intention of escaping IHT. My ex's mother left around £230,000; in those days the IHT threshold was £250,000. Too close for comfort, the

Revenue thought, so they came and investigated. It was nothing personal, but there was a strong possibility in their minds that my former mother-in-law had cleverly secreted some cash away before she died. In common with many people of her generation, Min, as we called her, was not used to handling money, and it would never for one single second have occurred to her to try to cheat the tax inspector – even if she had the remotest inkling of how she might do it.

It can be very upsetting, and add to the grief, when the Revenue acts as though the deceased was trying to cheat the system. In fact, the way that inheritance tax has to be handled so soon after death is one of the very worst aspects of this tax; you have to cope with it when you are in no fit state to do so, if an executor.

There are a number of guides now that you can buy that purport to tell you how to avoid paying inheritance tax. But the only way you can do this in reality is by making yourself much poorer while you are alive. Inheritance tax planning, however it is dressed up, comes down to one inescapable fact: in order to minimize or avoid IHT, you have to divest yourself of assets long before you die and, once they are divested, you are not allowed to make any use of them yourself. This is the stark reality.

And for most people, as for my late partner, John, giving away valuable assets while you are still alive will not be a viable option. When working out ways to minimize or avoid IHT you have to calculate whether the various ways of reducing IHT will cost you more than they are worth while you are alive and need the money. At least it can be argued you don't need the money when you are dead, although your heirs might be very glad of it.

But most of us possessing financial assets have a strong desire to pass them on to the next generation. This has always been the case – the 'One day this will all be yours' notion is deeply embedded in the DNA of all human beings. The number of SKI-ers, those intent on 'spending the kids' inheritance', is tiny compared to those who would like to pass on their assets without let or hindrance to their heirs.

For many older people no longer earning, the 'asset-rich, cash-poor' scenario is all too common. They simply cannot afford to give much money away while they are alive. There is also another important factor, which is that many people have severe misgivings about giving their assets away too quickly. Apart from the fact that they may need them for their own use in later life, there is another complication in that their adult children may divorce or separate – and then the ex gets a considerable slice of the assets already given away. It is this fact, possibly more than any other, that is making older homeowners extremely reluctant to reduce IHT by giving assets away when they are comparatively young themselves.

So – what does IHT mean for the average homeowner, and which are the best ways of circumventing or avoiding this tax being paid on death? And don't forget that IHT has to be paid before probate is granted, which means six months after death. If the tax cannot be paid, a loan has to be raised on the so far unsold or unrealized assets, which further reduces the amount the heirs will eventually receive after interest is paid on the loan.

And all saleable assets can be lumped into IHT, not just property. As seen with John's estate, even flat-pack furniture can count towards a deceased's assets. The Revenue people even have the power to come into the deceased's home to look at the walls for signs of recent removal of valuable paintings.

It is true that all can be passed without incurring IHT to the surviving spouse or registered civil partner, but only if you have made a will expressly stating this. If you have not made a valid will or not registered a civil partnership, the IHT rules will apply. For couples simply cohabiting, there is no escape. That much-despised 'piece of paper' – the wedding or civil partnership certificate – is vital to protecting your partner when you die, as the *only* exception with IHT is for those joined by law in an intimate relationship. Siblings, children and other relatives do not escape, either.

Supposing you have a house or house plus other assets worth in excess of the IHT threshold, what can you do?

These are your options:

- You can of course forget all about it and let your heirs or bene-ficiaries look after the fallout.

- You can downsize to give yourself some cash in the bank. This cash is still counted up with your other assets for IHT purposes when you die, but if you have enough money to pay IHT in the bank it will make life easier for your executors.

- You can consider equity release. You can sell your house, decide to rent instead and use the money released to live on.

- You can give away up to £3,000 a year without incurring any tax liability and also give away money, property, shares, paintings or other valuable assets seven years before you die. After this time, they become free of IHT but, if you die before this time, they will go back into your estate, on a sliding scale depending on how many years have elapsed since you gave them away, to be assessed for IHT.

- Or you can plan now and take out an insurance policy designed to cover any IHT bill your estate might incur. This policy will pay out the amount of tax incurred, before probate is granted.

But you cannot:

- Give your house to your children (or other beneficiaries) and continue to live in it yourself. This is known as a 'gift with reservation' and the Revenue has been on to it for some time. The only way this would work is if you paid your children a market rent for the property. Why can't you give your house to your children? Well, if this were an option, everybody would do it, and nobody would ever pay any IHT.

- Give all your money away while you are alive and go on to benefits, or live like a church mouse, in order to cheat the Exchequer. Again, they are on to this one. It used to be that you could divest yourself of your assets and live like a pauper, which is what the novelist Daphne du Maurier did in the 1970s, but no longer.

- Go and live abroad in the hope of avoiding IHT. You will still be liable, either in the home country or in the adopted country. Although you will most likely not have to pay tax twice, you – or your heirs – will almost certainly have to pay it once.

■ Tie up all your money in trusts to avoid IHT. Again, the Treasury is on to this one. In the March 2006 Budget the Chancellor infamously assaulted accumulation and maintenance trusts, which are often used to pass wealth down to grandchildren. Such trusts will now have to pay a slice of the capital to the Revenue when they are first established. At one time, there were specific provisions to exclude grandchildren from IHT liability and, accordingly, these trusts became extremely popular as they could be used to give grandchildren a useful start on the property ladder. But as the beneficial status of these trusts has now been removed, there is little advantage in setting them up any more.

But there are also more variables. Your IHT liability will be influenced not only by the sum of your financial assets, but also by your lifestyle and circumstances. It will make a difference whether you are single and living alone, are cohabiting, are in a first marriage, have remarried in later life, have a dependent child or children living with you, have retired or relocated abroad, or have a property portfolio, debts or mortgages. There is no overall scenario that fits everybody so, although it is a very simple tax for the Treasury to collect, it is extremely complicated to understand and to make sensible provision for its reduction. This is why a whole army of advisers and insurance products are now available, just to make things even more confusing.

Although the various housing options and their IHT implications will be discussed in detail in the following chapters, here is a brief guide to what you can and cannot do to minimize your IHT liability.

Husbands and wives, and those registered in a civil partnership, each have their own IHT allowance, even when the properties and other assets are jointly owned. This means that a couple could leave £570,000 without paying tax if each made use of his or her nil-rate band. In order to take advantage of the 'spouse exemption' you may first need to change ownership by changing to 'tenants in common' rather than 'joint tenants'. This needs a solicitor, so if you are married or in a civil partnership you would need to take legal advice on whether it is advantageous in your particular circumstances to change the wording of the ownership.

When you are 'tenants in common' you each own half the home, rather than owning it jointly, as 'one flesh'. Once you split ownership of your home, you need to draw up new wills leaving your share and your other assets in trust to your children. This is known as a 'nil-rate discretionary trust'.

But you cannot do this yourself or with just an informal arrangement. You need an expert familiar with this type of trust, and you can expect to pay in excess of £1,000 to set up the trust. Once set up, it will protect up to the current nil-rate band for IHT when the first partner dies, thus saving a six-figure tax sum. The surviving spouse is free to continue living in the house, and another benefit – especially as you get older – is that the council cannot take the value of your home into account when assessing you for means-tested benefits if you have to go into a care home. This is because you technically only own half a house, which is unsaleable on the open market.

Married people with children should definitely consider this option. It may not work, though, if you are in a second marriage and, in any case, you cannot do this if you are simply cohabiting, which is a lifestyle choice ever more people are now making.

If, as a married couple, you leave everything to each other and then your children when you die, your children will become liable for any inheritance tax unless you make use of this discretionary trust.

What you cannot do is to give your home to your children while you are still alive as 1) you would have to pay them a market rent to live there and 2) they could, if they liked, kick you out, sell the house and pocket the proceeds. Don't forget that IHT does not become payable until you die. If you continue to live in your house without paying a market rent, this is known as a 'gift with reservation' and will not enable you to avoid IHT.

In order to meet the seven-year rule, after which time all gifts become exempt from IHT, you need to have a clear paper trail proving when the gift was given. The best and simplest way of doing this is to write a letter to your child(ren) saying you have given them the money and how much it is, and also keep any bank records showing the money leaving your account on that day.

You can if you like give money to pay for your grandchildren's school fees, for instance, without it being regarded as IHT evasion, if the amounts you give do not compromise your own lifestyle in the meantime.

Ever more people are deciding to take out special insurance policies so that their heirs will not have to pay IHT, but as the premiums can be £200 or more a month you have to be sure that you can afford this going out of your account every month and that you are not likely to pay more in insurance premiums than your IHT liability. One big advantage of insurance is that at least the policy will pay the IHT on your death and your heirs will not lose out.

If you give or sell your home to your children or grandchildren, this may incur POAT – pre-owned assets tax – which was devised solely to plug any remaining holes in inheritance tax. POAT refers to the benefit you receive from an asset previously owned and is a pernicious tax that those attempting to circumvent IHT must now take on board.

Discretionary trust wills

As we have seen, all assets can be passed without incurring inheritance tax, and without having to resort to complicated schemes, between spouses and registered civil partners. IHT, though, must be paid when the remaining partner dies.

Discretionary trust wills remain one of the few legal ways of circumventing IHT, but they are only valid between spouses or civil partners. These wills make use of each partner's nil-rate band to minimize IHT on death. If the marital home is worth, say, £500,000, nothing is paid on the death of the first partner, but on the death of the second (assuming no other assets) there will be an IHT bill of around £90,000 to pay.

With a discretionary trust will, though, each partner makes use of his or her nil-rate band and puts the rest into a 'discretionary trust' whereby this amount of capital passes out of the hands of the survivor and will not be taxable on the death of the remaining partner.

If you are married or in a civil partnership and your house is worth more than £300,000, it would be worth considering a discretionary trust. It does cost quite a lot to set up this kind of trust, and it is also essential to talk to a solicitor who understands this kind of trust, as you cannot set it up in an informal way.

This type of trust only works, though, if you intend to leave your house and other assets in their entirety firstly to your partner and then to your children when the second partner dies. The main thing is to ensure that the remaining partner will not be short of money, if owning effectively only half a house.

It is not a suitable solution for everybody with estates in excess of the nil-rate band, and would not work in any case with cohabitees who are not married or in a civil partnership.

Warning! Probate and capital gains tax

Before probate is granted, every saleable asset must be valued by independent valuers. In the majority of cases, the most valuable asset anybody leaves will be property, and this must be valued at its current market value by an estate agent, who will present the valuation in writing. But, as we know, property values can change very quickly and, if the property is sold for a price greatly in excess of the valuation, capital gains tax may be payable by the beneficiaries. This is again to prevent properties being valued at less than their true worth for the purposes of minimizing inheritance tax.

This is something to bear in mind, as when estates are complicated it can take a year or more for probate to be granted, by which time any property still on the market could have increased considerably in value.

Nowadays, ordinary property-owning people who are not particularly sophisticated financially are tying themselves up in knots trying to leave as much as possible to their children or other beneficiaries, while enjoying a good lifestyle themselves while they are alive. Trying to avoid or minimize IHT can be a tricky balancing act, so we will delineate all the housing options now available in later life, while detailing the IHT implications of each choice.

2 Staying put

The biggest and most agonizing question looming over older homeowners these days is: should I stay or should I go? Is it better to remain in the house where you may have lived happily for many years or downsize to somewhere smaller, cheaper and more convenient?

A survey from the Bradford and Bingley Building Society in 2006 showed that 85 per cent of pensioners vastly preferred to stay put and only one in five homeowners would willingly consider downsizing. A quarter of respondents said they would go back to work rather than have to sell up to release equity. In this same survey, 68 per cent of pensioners owned properties with three or more bedrooms.

Mark Rees is a typical example. A single man in his 60s, he lives alone in a detached, three-bedroom house in Tunbridge Wells with a garage (although he doesn't have a car), and says: 'People are always advising me to move to somewhere smaller, but how do they know what's too big? If I did move, where would I put my grand piano, for instance? Also, I have lived in this house all my life and know the neighbours and the area. It's all very familiar and cosy for me.'

As we know, moving house is one of the more traumatic experiences of life and, in any case, few people enjoy uprooting, especially when they are very happy in their present quarters. The answer to the enormous question of whether to move or stay will probably involve a lot of heart-searching, but in addition a great deal of very detailed number-crunching will be necessary to determine whether it makes financial sense to stay in the same house. This is especially the case if the home is likely to become ever more unmanageable and expensive to maintain as time goes on. All properties need constant maintenance and there may not be the money or energy to carry out repairs as you get older.

If you decide you can comfortably afford to remain in the big family home and will also be able to comfortably afford possibly round-the-clock nursing care in years to come, should you need it, then you will probably not need much persuading to stay put. If in other people's opinion it is too big for you, well, that is really none of their business.

The novelist Daphne du Maurier insisted on remaining in her large, cold house in Par, Cornwall, to the end of her life, even when she was living there completely alone and needed full-time nursing care. Another old lady I know, now over 90, continues to live in the very large house with extensive grounds where she brought up her four children – even though her children are now themselves in their 60s and are considering downsizing or moving into sheltered housing. She needs permanent nursing care, which costs around £100,000 a year, but she is lucky enough to be able to afford it.

A couple in their 60s, still hale and hearty enough, have decided to remain in their eight-bedroom manor house with a large garden, orchard and many outbuildings because they 'can't be bothered' to look for somewhere smaller and more manageable. They love the house where they have lived for over 25 years and say they wouldn't know where to start looking or what to go for if they did decide to move.

The problems arise mainly when it is not going to be easy to carry on affording the family home and yet there is enormous reluctance to up sticks and go.

The difficulty of maintaining a home on a retirement pension has been the driving force behind the pensioners' marches and willingness to go to prison for unpaid council tax. In many areas of the country, council tax has become too high to be easily afforded by those on a fixed pension. Yet many of these rebellious pensioners are already living in houses not worth enough money to enable them to downsize to free up extra cash.

The usual advice for people rattling around in a house that has become too big, too unwieldy and too expensive is to downsize. This is what I did, and I ended up with a large lump sum in the bank. I am now living in a convenient flat. I could have carried on living in the house for many more years probably, but it seemed a good idea to sell up rather than have all the fuss and bother of maintaining a house that was too big for me on my own. But not all properties allow you to downsize and have money to spare once all the transactions are complete. It all depends on how much your home is worth in the first place and what you would have to spend on another property that would suit you. Then there are buying, selling and moving costs, which may seriously eat into any remaining nest egg.

There is another important factor to consider: a house that suits you very well when you are extremely fit and well at 60 may not be such a good bet when you are frail and ill at 80 and can no longer climb stairs or get into the bath unaided.

But what if you have absolutely no intention of moving, yet worry about being able to afford to stay on in your present home? There are a number of ways you can make money from your existing property while continuing to live in it, and one may be just right for you. You might be able, for instance, to:

■ rent out your garage or off-road parking space;

■ take in lodgers;

■ turn your home into a small B&B;

■ turn your home into two self-contained flats;

■ offer short lets;

■ take out equity release.

All these options will bring more money into your existing home and make life a little easier financially, but for every one there will be a price to pay in relinquishing some of your living or outside space, or ownership of at least part of your home.

Renting out your garage or car space

This is one of the easiest ways of making some useful extra money from your home, if your parking facility has become surplus to your own requirements. Depending on the area and demand, you can make up to £150 a week, with no work or effort whatever.

Obviously people have been doing this on an informal basis for many years, but now there is a dedicated website, www.parkat-myhouse.com, where you can advertise your space completely free. This site was set up in September 2006 with the intention of putting residents and drivers in touch with each other. Founder Anthony Eskanazi said: 'Many workers are keen to avoid the astronomical costs of all-day parking, and residents with a space can make useful money for no effort whatever.' Eskanazi had the idea of the website when in San Francisco. He kept seeing empty spaces beside residential properties, yet drivers had absolutely nowhere to park. He then thought: 'Why not utilize these empty spaces?' You can let out your car space to a grateful driver year round or just for specific events, such as Wimbledon tennis. Apart from putting your details on the website, you can advertise in local papers, newsagents' windows or other local facilities. Typical charges can be discovered by looking at the website.

So far as tax is concerned, strictly speaking you are supposed to declare this income to HMRC. If you just pocket cash, you risk being investigated for undeclared income, as the Revenue are now clamping down hard on people making pin money from their homes without declaring it.

Taking in lodgers

Homeowners have been taking in lodgers to make extra money for centuries, and this method of making financial use of a spare room is still highly popular. There always have been and always will be people who for one reason or another want to rent a room. My late partner, John Sandilands, wrote about what lodgings were like in the 1950s:

> Lodgings were invariably old, chilly and decorated in the style of a police barracks but they were swept and scoured and buffed as if to remove all traces of a fatal epidemic. This ferocious level of

cleanliness was tied in with the moral code of such establishments ~~which, although fractured with great regularity on the quiet, was~~ adhered to rigidly in public... What a breed they [landladies] were! In nearly every case, cruel fate had forced them into a course of action as desperate as taking in lodgers, as the gruesome phrase of the period described their plight.

(Lloyd's Log, November 1988)

But, like everything else in life, both the old-fashioned, traditional landlady beloved of 1950s novels, films and amusing articles, and the old-fashioned, traditional lodgings themselves have been updated somewhat. Many modern landladies do not provide meals or do their lodgers' washing, and nor do they grimly uphold a strict moral code. Instead, today's landladies are people – singles or couples – who want to make use of a spare room, and usually these days they do their utmost to ensure the comfort and well-being of their temporary housemates.

From a personality point of view, you have to be the sort of person who does not mind, or at least is able to put up with, strangers in your house who may possibly use your living room, bathroom and kitchen. To make the arrangement tolerable and workable, there must be a big enough kitchen to accommodate extra people and, ideally, any lodgers should have their own sitting room and bathroom. Many modern lodgers will have cars, so two or three car parking spaces are a definite plus, as well.

There must also be very strong demand for this kind of accommodation in your area. In locations where there are plenty of flats available to rent, there may be little demand for traditional-type lodgings.

Liz Anderson, who works as an IT expert at the Open University, is coming up to retirement. With this in mind, she decided to adapt the two spare rooms in her spacious bungalow near Cranfield University and take in lodgers. This, she believes, will enable her to remain in her house after retirement and at least enable her to pay bills. Liz says: 'It's a seller's market here because there are so many postgraduate students coming from all over the world, no flats or apartments in the area, and very few halls of residence.' In 2007, Liz charges each of her two lodgers £300 a month and does not provide meals, cleaning or other services. She adds:

> I keep a rent book because I have to declare the income, but they pay me in cash. As they are mainly foreigners, this is usually easier for them than setting up standing orders. I take a deposit of one month's rent plus a month's rent in advance, but although it's a cash deal I always give them a receipt. The rooms they use have to be able to work as study bedrooms, so they must have lots of storage, a single bed, a desk and – most importantly for students – broadband connection.

Liz does not provide bedding and does not clean the lodgers' rooms, although she has a weekly cleaner for the bathroom, kitchen and common areas. In the kitchen, the lodgers each have their own fridge and storage cupboards and they share a freezer. They use the communal washing machine and tumble dryer. They also have their individual cupboards in the bathroom. Liz has her own private sitting room where the lodgers are not allowed, but they have their own lounge with satellite television. In common with most present-day landladies, Liz does not allow smoking, and the lodgers are not allowed to use the house telephone. She says:

> I would not dream of taking lodgers off the street I didn't know anything about, and nor would I take undergraduates. My lodgers are all either PhD or MBA students of average age 30 and they are here for a specific purpose and a specific length of time. They are just here to work, not live an undergraduate-type student life.

A plus with taking students is that you are not liable for extra council tax, as you would be with working adults or retired people. The government encourages people to make use of spare rooms and, under its Rent-a-Room scheme, you are allowed tax-free rent of up to £4,250 a year. This relief is available for furnished rooms in your own home and no expenses are claimable. It is up to you to work out whether you are better off claiming this relief or paying tax in the normal way and claiming expenses. In Liz Anderson's case, she pays tax on the £2,950 not covered by the relief.

If you have a mortgage, you should inform your lender and also your insurer, as you may not be covered on ordinary household insurance for extra people. Lodgers are responsible for insuring their own belongings.

You do not have to be a homeowner to rent out a room, but if you are renting your home yourself or are on a lease you must check that taking in lodgers is allowed. This type of letting does not incur capital gains tax liability when you come to sell. Another advantage, especially if you live alone, is that having lodgers provides greater security and deters opportunistic burglars, who typically target older people living alone.

Many universities, colleges and language schools have websites giving details of accommodation needs, and most provide guidelines for their student hosters.

Turning your home into a small B&B

This could be an option if you have a lovely home in a popular tourist or resort area. The B&B business is thriving, but before involving yourself in any expense regarding conversion or adaptation you would need to do your research to check out the competition, level of market and potential occupancy rates, and what you could charge. You would probably need to guarantee 75 per cent year-round occupancy to make the project finan-cially viable.

You would also have to check out health and safety issues and the question of a liquor licence and decide whether you will serve evening meals. These days, all bedrooms must be en suite, and you will also definitely have to obtain planning permission for change of use.

Jill and John Hitchins run a B&B in their beautiful old-rectory home near the quaint, vibrant town of Totnes, Devon – a highly popular tourist area. Totnes is famous as a hippy, alternative type of town and, because of this reputation, attracts visitors from all over the world. Jill, formerly a TV producer, and John, a college lecturer, felt that setting up the B&B was a better option than moving to a smaller place now that their two children have grown up and gone. The Old Rectory has three letting rooms, and they are in the process of creating a fourth, from a downstairs storage room. Jill is a Leith's-trained cook and one of her delights is to be able to offer gourmet evening meals. She says:

> Although the house is much too big for just the two of us, we couldn't bear the thought of moving. But apart from its size, there was also the fact that it was not going to be easy to afford it when John retired and I was no longer working. When we sat down and thought about it, we realized that the house would lend itself beautifully to a B&B as there are six bedrooms and a two-acre garden.
>
> There are two staircases, so we did not need fire doors, which was a relief, as those horrible doors would have completely spoilt the look of the house. We do make a profit although the business does not make enough money to live on by itself. But we could not afford to stay here without the B&B.

Jill felt that a liquor licence was essential, so they applied for and obtained this – in itself quite a business. They have to have a hygiene inspection every year and also had to offer disabled access. They employ one full-time member of staff; otherwise Jill does all the cooking and shopping herself. They are full for most of the year and also do events such as weddings and anniversaries.

Setting up a B&B means that your home is now partly a commercial enterprise, and this will certainly attract capital gains tax when you sell. If you are intending to stay there for the rest of your life, the capital gains tax element can be discounted, as this is not paid after death. But while running the B&B, you will have to pay business rates instead of ordinary council tax, and business rates, of course, are more than council tax.

But you also have to be aware that turning your home into a B&B could make it lose value on the open market. Jill and John believe that their house is worth less as a B&B than it would be as a family home. But, as they are not intending to sell in the fore-seeable future, this is not an aspect that concerns them.

Turning your home into two self-contained flats

Obviously, your home has to be big enough and of a suitable type of design to allow this, but it can be a good way of combining staying where you are with producing useful income from the part of the house no longer being used.

One of my friends, a literary agent, owns a large terraced house in fashionable Notting Hill, West London. After her three children had grown up and left home, she decided to turn her basement – which had once been her office – into a self-contained one-bedroom flat. This needed minimal building work, as the basement already had its own front and back door, although planning permission and building consent were needed. The heating and utilities had to be separated, as my friend wanted the flat to be self-contained enough to be able to let it on an assured shorthold tenancy.

The basement flat, now let, not only yields a good income because of its extremely popular location, but also provides her with useful options, should she need them in later life. At the moment, she herself is living in the main part of the house and there is still plenty of room for her to put up her adult children and their partners – although not all at once. But if her circumstances change drastically and all of her authors suddenly stop earning (dread the thought!), she could herself move to the basement and let out the main house for a large sum of money.

The good thing about the separate flats option is that the tenants are completely self-contained, and you need never see them at all. If my friend wanted to make a lot of money, she could even sell off the basement flat on a separate lease. Or she could sell the main house and keep the basement for herself. Obviously, this would be quite complicated, would require a new Land Registry entry and would need legal documentation. But one way or another, it means she need never move from the house and location she loves. Trendy shops are just opposite, as is the bus stop, and the tube is just up the road. So – everything is near at hand, and this becomes increasingly important with age.

So far as tax is concerned, obviously all income from the rental flat has to be declared, although there are expenses that can be set against this income. When and if my friend comes to sell, there could be capital gains tax liability on the part of the property that has been used for income. This is something that would need taxation advice before you proceed, as it could also affect inheritance tax. You would also need permission from your mortgage lender to convert your house in this way, if you have a mortgage.

Offering short lets

Another way of making money from your home, especially if you are away a lot, is to offer short lets while you are not in the house yourself. Again, there is a thriving business in short lets and it can be extremely profitable, as your tenant, or guest, pays a premium for the privilege of living in a private home for such a short time.

You have to bear in mind, though, that these lets are technically subject to approval by the local authority, as some do not allow lets of less than three months in case it takes away from the area's hotel trade.

Your home also, of course, has to be suitable for letting to upmarket holidaymakers, and it must comply with all current legislation. There must be a current gas safety certificate and landlord's electrical safety certificate in place, at least if you are letting it through a recognized agency. As with taking in lodgers, broadband connection is essential, as is satellite and terrestrial television.

Your property must also be fully equipped and ready to let, and all kitchenware, crockery and linen must be provided. The home must be as well set up as a hotel and there must be hanging space and drawer space for guests' clothes. You would also have to draw up a detailed inventory and have the property professionally cleaned before each let.

Choosing this option means you must keep your house as clean and neat as a five-star hotel and, although guests are paying for a private home that will have some evidence of occupation, they also want the place to be clutter-free.

The letting agent, should you use one, will normally deduct income tax at source before paying you, in addition to the letting fee. Again, if you have a mortgage, you must inform your mortgage lenders and insurers, to check that you are covered. There are now many agencies operating this type of let and they will usually give detailed guidelines and also come and inspect your home, to see if it is suitable.

Some homeowners determined to stay put decide to rent out their homes in this way when they go on holiday, and the extra cash often enables them to carry on affording the place when they are no longer earning. You would not normally incur capital gains tax on this type of let when you come to sell, unless you do it as a full-time business or at your second home.

But – your present home may not easily lend itself to any of the above options. There is also the fact that, apart from renting out a car space, all the ways of making extra money from your property involve you in some extra expense in the first place and having strangers in your home. It costs money to convert homes into places suitable for lodgers, to equip them for short lets or to set up a bed and breakfast. In some cases, these costs cannot be met out of capital and it may be difficult to get a loan.

Taking out equity release

If you would prefer to stay in your home but cannot or do not want to adapt it to a money-making enterprise, you might consider commercial equity release. This is a financial product that enables you to stay in your home at the same time as pocketing some cash from its value. Equity release has gained in popularity over the past few years as house prices have increased so much and as ever more people live to vast old ages.

The problem is, many older people no longer working will have a struggle to make ends meet if they remain in their home. In the Bradford and Bingley survey referred to at the beginning of the chapter, non-retired respondents had on average an annual income of £25,700; this went down to an average of £11,700 a year on retirement. In 2007, it is estimated that you need an income of at least £18,000 a year to enjoy a comfortable retirement.

For many people facing retirement and determined not to move house, equity release may be their only answer. The Financial Services Authority (FSA) has stated that, in the main, people looking for equity release are 'vulnerable' as they have reduced earning power after retirement and do not own homes valuable enough to make downsizing a viable option. For this reason, the FSA has been working hard in recent years to regulate this sector and to ensure that only those with detailed knowledge of equity release should be allowed to give advice.

This scheme releases cash that enables you to afford to carry on living in your home as well as carrying out improvements from time to time. Equity release is aimed at the 60-plus homeowner with no remaining mortgage who is asset-rich and cash-poor and who does not want the bother, upheaval and financial strain of moving. The scheme enables you to afford to stay in your home by giving you either a lump sum or monthly income raised from the value of your property.

At the same time, for many homeowners, it has the effect of completely wiping out inheritance tax. Sounds good?

There are two main types of equity release scheme: a lifetime mortgage, a product that has long been regulated by the FSA, and a home reversion plan, which has been regulated by the FSA since April 2007. Although home reversion providers have been quick to point out that there has not been any evidence of unfair dealing or mis-selling, the sector's self-regulating body, the Safe Home Income Plans (SHIP), eventually felt that home reversions should be regulated in the same way as lifetime mortgages. In the past, home reversion plans have not qualified for regulation as they have been seen as property purchases rather than mortgages. The main reason for the regulation is to make sure all advisers are fully conversant with the ramifications of home reversion schemes before giving advice, as they are a complicated product.

Lifetime mortgage scheme

With this, your home is used as security for a loan that is repaid, with high interest rolled up and added, on the property's sale when you die or move into long-term care. A lifetime mortgage is exactly what it says it is, a mortgage that lasts a lifetime. This means it never ends.

In one variation of the lifetime mortgage scheme you borrow a sum secured on the present value of your house and you are charged interest each month on the loan. But you will also have a lump sum to spend or invest as you wish, and this will more than cover the amount borrowed. The amount you borrow when you take out the lifetime mortgage is fixed, so that any increase in the value of your home will belong to you or your family. You can borrow at a fixed rate so that you know exactly what you will be paying each month. Although lifetime mortgages never end, they can be useful for very elderly people who may not have much longer to live.

In the past, lifetime mortgages could mean that the house eventually went into negative equity and this meant that the home, far from being an asset, became a liability on which the deceased's heirs had to pay the mortgage lender. Most schemes nowadays promise not to go into negative equity, however long the recipient of the equity release might live.

Most companies offering lifetime mortgages belong to SHIP, which regulates terms and conditions. In this case, the money you borrow has to be used to buy an annuity that guarantees you an income for life, and mortgage payments are automatically deducted from this monthly income. The original capital is repaid from the sale proceeds after you die. As the income is fixed at the outset of the plan, it may be eroded by inflation if you live long enough.

The problem with built-in annuities is that they are not a particularly competitive financial product and are equally low everywhere. Also, interest rates on mortgage-based schemes are usually higher than on an ordinary mortgage.

With a lump sum lifetime mortgage scheme, the interest is rolled up over the number of years of the loan and repaid, together with the original amount borrowed, when the property is sold. The remaining proceeds, if any, form part of your estate but, as the period of the loan is unknown, the amount of final debt cannot be guaranteed and the outstanding loan together with compound interest can grow substantially.

On an income lifetime mortgage scheme, you get a previously agreed tax-free monthly income for the rest of your life. The interest grows more slowly with this type of scheme, as interest is charged only on the amount you borrow at the time.

There are a few other variations on the lifetime mortgage scheme, such as a drawdown scheme where you can draw on funds as and when you may need them; a protected equity scheme whereby you can ensure the debt will not exceed more than a certain percentage of the property's value; and the fixed option scheme, which offers a known repayment figure from the outset and is not affected by the life of the loan or how long you may live.

Lifetime mortgages can be taken on either a fixed interest rate or a variable interest rate. A fixed rate is, as the name suggests, fixed at the outset and will not alter, whereas a variable rate, though often cheaper at the outset, could increase or decrease according to Bank of England interest rates during the life of the loan.

Home reversion schemes

These work slightly differently in that you sell part of your home to an investment company in exchange for a cash sum. When the property is sold, either before or after your death, the proceeds are split between that company and you or your heirs. If you are struggling to live on a small pension and cannot in any case afford to move elsewhere, a scheme like this can make sense.

But don't imagine you will be able to sell part of your home for what it is worth, as the reversion company will only pay you a percentage of the current market value. Suppose you have a home valued at £200,000 and want to sell 50 per cent of it to a reversion company. You will be lucky to get £40,000 for that percentage. The amount you get can be paid either in a lump sum or as a monthly income. The advantages of home reversion schemes are that there are no monthly payments to make and your family will know at the outset what share of your home they will be inheriting on your death, although not the actual amount. The reversion company makes its money when your property is sold, so may have to wait a long time for it.

But even if your home does not go up a penny in value between the time of taking out a home reversion scheme and your death, the reversion company will still have made a profit of £60,000 on your £200,000 home. Whichever way you look at it, the reversion company will get the lion's share of the value of your home – say, 70 or 80 per cent of its worth, at the very least – because in addition to only paying you a percentage of your share when the scheme is set up, the reversion company is also clever enough to pay you, or your heirs, only a proportion of the eventual sale price of your remaining share of the property. The reason stated for this is that the company may have to wait many years to get its hands on the money. The company also pockets any increase in capital growth in that time. So, if your £200,000 home is worth £400,000 by the time it is sold, the reversion company stands to rake in a handy £300,000 or so profit – depending on the agreed share it will pay out on the sale.

When home reversion schemes are set up, the title deeds are transferred to the provider.

Peter Couch, Managing Director of Bridgewater Equity Release, which has been providing equity release plans since the mid-1990s, explains how home reversion works:

> The home reversion provider pays the customer a lump sum at the start of the plan. The provider then has to wait for many years before receiving an unknown return at an unknown date in the future, usually 10–20 years later. The potential future value of the property plus the possible life expectancy of the customer are both taken into account when drawing up the plan, although of course we cannot predict either completely accurately. The cash payment is usually between 40 and 60 per cent of the current open market value of the proportion of the property being sold, and the customer then has the option of taking a lump sum or income. All these issues must be discussed with the customer before the plan is put into action.
>
> In return for the sale of part of the home, the customer receives a lifetime lease for that proportion. No rent is paid, and the scheme enables the customer to leave a legacy on death. With a lifetime mortgage, the equity in the home can go down to nothing if the

customer lives long enough. We believe that home reversion plans can offer a better deal than lifetime mortgages.

Why should a homeowner choose a home reversion plan over a lifetime mortgage? Peter Couch says:

> If you are looking for certainty, then a home reversion scheme will be better. You make a decision to sell a proportion of your home to us but you will not get the true value of that proportion.
>
> What you do get is an assurance that you won't be turned out, and if in the future you want to sell another percentage of your home then you can do that if you like. The whole point of home reversion is that you the customer are passing on the risk to us.

With both schemes, there will also be valuation and legal fees to pay, and you will be required to have – and pay for – a survey. There could be in addition set-up fees of around £500–£600. Once the scheme is set up, you will be required to keep the place in reasonable condition and there may be regular inspections to ensure this is being done. Most companies inspect every three years, and Peter Couch says:

> You are required to keep the house in good repair with all equity release schemes. In practice, this is not usually a problem as the generation now taking out equity release respect their homes and like to look after them. The thing is, it is still their home and they remain proud of it. If in years to come they lose mental capacity and are no longer capable of maintaining their property, we will offer support. You still have the right to live there for the rest of your life.

Peter Couch believes it is 'arrogant' of some people to suggest that older people should move to a smaller home instead of taking out an equity release plan, which will enable them to remain in the family home.

You would normally be able to release 15 to 55 per cent of the present value of your property, depending on age and health. The older you are, the greater the amount of equity that can be released.

Equity release schemes are certainly not charitable enterprises, but extremely hard-headed ways of making money out of elderly people's homes. In order to be eligible for them, you usually have to be aged 60 or more and own your home outright, which must be in reasonable condition. You cannot take out this type of scheme if you are a leaseholder with fewer than 75 years left on the lease (which is the case with many older homeowners in leasehold properties) or if you have a mobile or park home, live above commercial premises or have a registered smallholding. Suitable homes must be of standard traditional bricks and mortar. Money released has to be from your main home and cannot come from a second or holiday home. It comes free of tax, but any interest received from investing the cash will be taxable.

Your spouse or partner can carry on living in the home after your death, so long as his or her name is on the title deeds. If the spouse's name is not on the title deeds, which is the case with many elderly people who just put the husband's name on the deeds, you may have a problem. Adult children residing with you may not be able to carry on living in the home after your death. Again, if this is your situation, you would need to discuss it with an equity release provider before signing up.

Are these schemes a good idea? Most personal finance experts are of the opinion that you should only consider equity release as a last resort, not as a first choice. Although the equity release business, which used to have a very bad name indeed, has considerably cleaned up its act, it is also the case that you never really get much money from these schemes and you lose much of the saleable value of your house at the same time.

Adult children on the whole do not like their parents taking out equity release schemes as their own inheritances will be inevitably diminished. That is why some schemes are advertised as wiping out IHT. But demand is steadily growing, particularly among those people for whom downsizing is not a realistic option.

Under the scheme, you will be responsible for keeping up the home's value by repairing and maintaining it. You will still have to pay all utilities and council tax. But there is more: if you are in receipt of state benefits, you could lose these once you take out a scheme, as the extra income you receive may put you above the benefits level. If this is your situation, you have to work out very carefully indeed whether you would be significantly better off under the scheme. Where money is tight, you may be better off claiming means-tested benefits, if you are eligible.

There may also be penalties if you want, or need, to move into sheltered housing later, and some schemes do not allow you to transfer to another property. And because the mortgage never stops on the lifetime mortgage scheme, it could mean that the cost of borrowing, say, £80,000 on a property worth £350,000 will incur a repayment of £256,000 being demanded after 20 years.

With equity release, you have to be very sure you will never want to move, as if you do you may not have much of a house to sell any longer. The schemes are not suitable for short-term loans, and if your home desperately needs repairs you may be entitled to grants from your local authority or cheap loans from the non-profit-making Home Improvement Trust, for instance. This trust is especially designed to provide low-cost loans to older people secured against the value of the home.

If you are still interested, these are the main questions to ask:

- How much could you end up owing?

- Are you ever likely to owe more than the value of your home?

- What kind of inheritance are you likely to be able to leave your heirs?

- If you are married, what will happen to your spouse on your death? The survivor may need to find alternative accommodation.

Patrick Collinson, the acerbic personal finance writer, believes that equity release is far from being the guaranteed safety net that many older homeowners imagine. A *Which?* report in 2006 concluded that equity release was a 'last resort' for pensioners and, commenting on this report, Collinson wrote in the *Guardian* (28 January 2006): 'Before ever embarking on any financial scheme, ask how many mouths it is going to have to feed. In an equity release scheme, you will pay commission to an adviser, solicitor, fees to a lender, plus the rolled-up interest. That is a lot of mouths.'

Alternatively, by selling your house and moving to somewhere smaller, the only mouth you are feeding is your own. Collinson continued:

> But what is extraordinary is how few retired people are willing to trade down, however sensible such a move may be. Survey after survey reveals that pensioners want to stay in their homes until they are carried out in a box.
>
> Over the years, we will build a colossal, expensive and unnecessary equity release industry to allow people to remain in their homes way past any rational reason for doing so. At the same time, we will force first-time buyers into ever tinier starter homes, and ask the same hard-pressed families to subsidise the council tax of elderly single pensioners in big, under-used properties.

Such people, he concludes, are foolhardy to view equity release as the pain-free way to remain in their homes.

A cautionary tale about equity release

In 1982, Mark Rees's mother took out an equity release scheme on her previously mortgage-free home in Tunbridge Wells, Kent. At the time Mark was living with her, as he had been unable to get a job and was on benefits.

Mrs Rees died in 1988, aged 81, and in 2007 her son, Mark, who is still living in the house, is struggling to pay off the 25-year mortgage he inherited when his mother died. He said:

> This scheme has been the most terrible thing ever. It gave Mum about £70 a month extra money, which hardly made any difference as she then lost her council tax benefit.
>
> Like most people of her generation who didn't know much about money, Mum was impressed by the men at the bank in suits and ties, talking smoothly to her. The equity release company wanted me to move out when Mum died, especially as I was then

on benefits. But I managed to get a mortgage, which the taxpayer paid until I was back in work and which I am still paying out of my earnings as a college lecturer.

Mark added: 'I would not have minded if Mum had got some decent financial benefit from the equity release, but she never did. When Mum died, I had the choice of selling the house for much less than it was worth, because of the equity release, or paying a 25-year mortgage on a previously mortgage-free house.' Mark advises: 'Anybody considering equity release should think very carefully if they have dependent children or others not named on the title deeds, living permanently with them, as these people will be homeless when the equity release recipient dies.'

It seems to me that equity release plans are most suitable for, say, a 75-year-old single person with no heirs who wants to remain in his or her home but needs a sizeable cash injection right now. For such a person, the possible value of the home after death is of no real interest.

How can equity release reduce inheritance tax?

When you take out an equity release plan, of whatever type, you are inevitably reducing the value of your home. But you have to be sure that the amount of interest you pay on the loan – or your estate pays – does not come to more than the inheritance tax saved. With me so far?

Here is an example that will clarify the issue. Suppose you are aged 75 and have a fully owned home worth £400,000. You borrow £100,000 through a lifetime mortgage. This automatically reduces the equity in your home to £300,000 – the amount you can leave to your heirs without incurring IHT in 2007.

Your £100,000 windfall can be spent or given away. If you have two children, say, and give them each £50,000, this will become free of IHT if you live for another seven years, and means you can help your children when they need it, without them having to wait until you die. But you must spend the money or give it away to reduce the IHT. If you just keep it in the bank, it will count towards your IHT liability.

But – and it's a big but – you will be charged interest on the £100,000 released. This is rolled up, added to the debt and must be paid from the estate when you die. After seven years, this debt will have grown to £50,000 at an average interest rate of 6 per cent. So you will be charged £50,000 interest to save £40,000 inheritance tax. A good deal? Not if you are doing it purely to beat the Revenue, only if you want to give money now to a child or grandchild to put into property.

Lifetime mortgages are usually available to those aged over 60 but experts warn that, if you borrow too early, the amount of debt that builds up will far exceed the inheritance tax saving. An interest rate of 6 per cent would result in the debt doubling in about 12 years.

An equity release debt is paid when you sell up, move into long-term care (see Chapter 8) or die.

The other type of equity release plan, home reversion schemes, are now regulated, but experts believe they are too expensive to enable you to make savings on IHT.

To sum up, you will only get a small percentage of your house's true value with equity release, and it can often completely wipe out the family inheritance. As against this, equity release can give a considerable, and immediate, cash bonus to otherwise hard-up pensioners. If you have not been able to save up much money for your retirement and your only real asset is your home, then it might well be better to take out a lifetime mortgage or home reversion scheme, to give you enough cash to live on.

The kinds of homeowners who most often consider equity release are those who would not in reality be able to downsize and buy a cheaper home, since the new home they buy would cost as much as the one they are selling.

Note: Equity release is a *very* profitable enterprise for insurance companies, banks and other financial institutions. As such, it is highly advertised and seductively presented. You can usually get a completely free guide to how equity release works from these institutions, most of which will also willingly send a smartly dressed representative (salesperson) round to your house to discuss it with you. If you send off for a guide, you can also expect endless telephone calls from salespeople following up on your enquiry.

As with any product that is sold hard, do not send off for a guide or invite a salesperson into your home unless and until you are pretty sure that this is what you want. In other words, make up your mind first and then contact the financial institution selling the product.

Because the schemes are complicated and vary according to your individual circumstances, it is a good idea to speak to an adviser from a SHIP-regulated company – so long as you remain aware that these advisers are, above all, salespeople who are trying to sell you a product on which they will earn a fat commission.

If you do want to stay in your own home, there is an organization, HOOP (Housing Options for Older People), that will appraise the situation and assess all the provisions available for help and support. Although sheltered housing is increasingly available, this entails moving, and often to a completely unknown area. It is a fact that the older you become the more difficult it is to uproot, however unsuitable your home may have become.

There are now many services to help older people stay in their homes, from meals on wheels to home helps, community wardens and home improvement agencies that will carry out repairs at low cost. HOOP says it is more difficult to make sensible housing choices in later life because of uncertainties around personal circumstances (illness and death, for instance) and lack of knowledge about support. It can also be difficult for older people actually to go and view new homes, apart from which the kind of property that most suits their needs may be unaffordable.

HOOP will send you a detailed questionnaire, which enables them to make a comprehensive assessment of your current housing and identify any information about solutions or alternatives.

Inheritance tax implications of staying put

IHT is basically a tax levied on the sum total of an individual's monetary assets after death, and it makes no difference whether you rent out rooms, divide up your house or take out equity release when you are alive. If your assets exceed the nil-rate band there will be IHT to pay at 40 per cent above that limit. IHT is the *only* tax paid after death and, in order to calculate it, your executors will have to add together everything that constitutes your estate.

If you are married or in a registered civil partnership (not an informal arrangement) and expect your estate to exceed the nil-rate band, you should contact your solicitor at once and discuss the best ways to write a will or set up a trust to minimize this payment, bearing in mind that there is a spouse exemption for IHT, which becomes payable on the death of the surviving spouse.

But if you are simply cohabiting or have adult children living with you, IHT will kick in and the property will have to be sold on your death. This could leave survivors homeless, so again it is something you need to discuss in plenty of time with your solicitor. When my partner died, I inherited our joint properties according to the terms of his will, but their value was still included in the IHT assessment. There was simply no way of circumventing this. In our case, none of the shared properties was my main home, so there was no question of being turned out. We were also lucky in that there was enough cash in the account to pay IHT without having to sell any properties first. Most people are not in this fortunate position.

Taking out equity release will seriously erode the value of your estate so that IHT may not be payable. Even so, if you are married, cohabiting or have dependent children living with you, it is essential to find out from the equity release company what the situation regarding this will be after the death of the property owner.

You can also use equity release to help your own children while you are alive. One author contact took out equity release in order to help his divorcing daughter buy a property. He fulfilled the age requirements and felt this was better than making her wait until after his death and possibly having to pay IHT on the estate.

3 Downsizing

As we saw in the previous chapter, more than three-quarters of retired people consider their home to be their 'castle' and are extremely reluctant to move or to consider downsizing. This can be the case even when they are continuing to live in homes with seven or eight bedrooms, or when the house has become completely unsuitable for their needs.

It can be impossible to overestimate the amount of emotion that may be tied up in a much-loved family home and, for this reason, house doctor Ann Maurice always advises people never to sell until they have mentally said goodbye to their home and are ready to leave it. Also, the prospect of moving when you have a lifetime's worth of clutter in the attic or garage can be so daunting that the dreaded day keeps being put off. We all have examples of elderly relatives who refused ever to throw anything away 'in case it comes in useful' and eventually the job of clearing everything out was left to their survivors, by which time everything unceremoniously went to the nearest council dump.

But if you do feel you are ready for a new home and a new challenge, downsizing is often a sensible way to free up useful money without putting yourself through all the lifelong hassle that signing up for a complicated financial product such as equity release produces. Never forget that, whenever you sign up to a financial product, you are in perpetual hock to the providers of that product, whether it is some form of loan, insurance, pension or mortgage. After you have signed up, things are now out of your control. You as an individual have no influence over interest rates, stock market rises or falls, earthquakes in one part of the world affecting oil prices in another part, or financial institutions going bust.

But, if you simply downsize and free up some cash from the sale of your house, you can put the money in the bank or under the mattress, spend it on a round-the-world cruise or invest in a buy-to-let. The choice is yours, and there is no super-slick sales-person gaining fat commission.

Some of the more sensible older homeowners may feel that to have a lot of cash tied up in bricks and mortar is basically dead money that could be better invested or spent elsewhere, bearing in mind that downsizing will usually entail a major change of lifestyle as well. And although some homeowners may feel a strong emotional pull to the old house, there are others who are only too glad to say goodbye to a home that no longer suits them and that, in any case, constitutes an expensive empty nest.

If you are considering downsizing from the too-large family house into something smaller and more manageable, what should you bear in mind? Do you have to decide exactly where you want to go and what kind of property you now want before starting the process?

I would say not necessarily. A friend of mine decided to downsize from a valuable, but somewhat dilapidated, house and put it on the market before he had found somewhere else to live. He was nearing 70 and not too well, and did not want the expense and upheaval of major renovation. In any case, he did not have the ready cash for the kind of work needed. He sold his house quickly in its unmodernized state and moved into rented accommodation for a year while looking around and making his mind up. By this strategy, he was able to give himself time to find exactly what suited him. Now that there is so much rented accommodation around, this can be a sensible plan if you know you want to downsize but have not made up your mind about your next home.

In any case, I would say you should give yourself at least a year to make it all work, declutter the house and make an informed decision about your next abode and location. Never downsize in a hurry, especially if you have accumulated lots of stuff over the years and are not totally clear about where to go next.

Before anything else, start getting rid of unwanted or long-piled-up stuff. This can in itself take a year, especially if you have never seriously decluttered before. You may have 30 or 40 years' worth of stuff stored away and not looked at for decades. Indeed, many older people are frightened of downsizing simply because they cannot face attacking their long-accumulated junk (or prized possessions, whichever way you look at it). Once you have taken a deep breath and made a start, throw out all the really useless items such as broken umbrellas, non-erectable children's tents, long-abandoned toys, chipped china and electrical items that no longer work. Then decide what you want to do with items you no longer want, but that have some value. You may be able to sell them at auction or on eBay.

When my late partner, John Sandilands, downsized, he carefully researched all the possible outlets for his superfluous goods such as old records, postcards, pieces of fabric, theatre programmes, old calendars, model soldiers and vehicles and either took them to suitable auction houses or advertised them for sale. In the first year he did this, he made £34,000 from his previously unconsidered trifles. Talk about cash in the attic! Books went to second-hand bookshops, furniture to furniture auctions, and paintings and pictures to relevant art sales. It was a lot of work but at the same time quite enjoyable. And the cash he realized from the sale of his collections, most of which had been mouldering in the attic and not even looked at for decades, was even more welcome. Some items of family interest were donated to members of his family who would appreciate them and, when finally all the stuff with any remaining value had been sold or donated, the rest went to the tip.

This process took 18 months but then John was a famous hoarder. But the point is that all the decluttering happened long before he had put his house up for sale or even looked at alternatives. By the time his house went on the market, it was ready to sell, with no excessive clearing out to be done.

But, whatever you do, *don't* just transfer the junk from your attic into a self-storage unit. All over the country, nay, all over the world, huge storage units on the edge of towns are full of clutter people can't quite bring themselves to throw away and yet that has no value or use either to themselves or to anybody else. The result is that the clutter stays in the storage unit maybe for years, at huge and ever-increasing cost. An average storage unit costs around £80 a month, which adds up to an awful lot of money over the years. Then you can't bear to visit it and face the business of clearing the storage unit. So there it expensively sits. Only use these units strictly on a short-term basis. Self-storage units are an extremely useful facility, but only if you can discipline yourself to throw away or sell most of your clutter first.

Mostly, your adult children will most definitely not want your furniture and accumulated items, especially little knick-knacks, statuettes, figurines and all the other artefacts they have profoundly hated over the years. One friend, when looking after her 90-year-old mother, sighed: 'Her house is absolutely full of knick-knacks. How can I tell her that we only want to see the back of them? She keeps talking about which items she will give me, which to each of my sisters, but none of us would give any of them houseroom for a minute.'

The other sad thing is that, usually, old furniture is simply not worth much. When I was clearing a house after a relative's death, I could not sell or even give the furniture away. Eventually, a house clearance firm came to take it away, at a price. Most people these days hate mahogany bookcases, walnut wardrobes and oak sideboards and, unless such furniture is genuinely antique, it has no value whatsoever.

The next thing is to get your home into a fit condition to sell. These days, house doctors, home stagers and declutter experts abound, and they are all making a living advising house vendors on ways to maximize their sale price. The problem is, they don't all agree with each other. Some home stagers recommend scouring your house of everything personal before putting it on the market, on the basis that purchasers are not buying your lifestyle, simply your house, whereas other experts advise a little sweet disorder and untidiness, so the place does not look too scoured and characterless. After years of clinical 'house doctoring', the advice is changing, particularly when it comes to putting the family home on the market.

Propertypriceadvice founder Louisa Fletcher says:

A lot of older people who downsize have money tied up in the property where they have lived for maybe 25 years, but not much money in the bank. Therefore, I would advise giving the place a thoroughly good professional spring clean but probably not spend much on redecoration and renovation. In the best scenario, you are only likely to get back what you spent on the place, rather than make a big profit from updating. A lick of paint over the worst parts will freshen it up, but if you spend £20,000 on a new kitchen and bathroom, you would be lucky to get that back on the sale.

Most potential buyers of homes where owners are downsizing are youngish families who, more than anything else, want space and location rather than a wonderfully smart renovated house. 'Many older people do not want the fuss and bother of modernizing a house just to sell it, even if they do have the money', says Louisa. 'If the house is in a desirable road and all the others have been extended or renovated, potential buyers will be able to see the possibilities. They will know that money is coming into the street.'

Louisa's mother, in her 60s, lives in one of the most desirable roads in Ringwood, Hampshire, but her bungalow, unlike most of the others in the street, has not been renovated, extended or improved. Louisa says:

My mum doesn't want to improve and extend her house but her bungalow will still command the top price because buyers can see from looking at others in the street that it will be easy to get planning permission for extending and going up in the loft.

If buyers can see that the other houses in the street have been improved, that gives them the confidence to buy, even though they may themselves be buying an unmodernized place. If you live in a hotspot you can hang on for the top price, whatever the condition of your own place.

This advice is echoed by Tracy Kellett, who runs a home-finding agency in Henley, Berkshire. She says:

About 80 per cent of our clients looking for family homes want something they can do up, rather than a place already absolutely perfect but maybe not to their taste. In fact, many people nowadays will pay *more* for a place that needs doing up, as they can then put their own personality into it.

Our clients get very excited about going into an old person's house as that's what they want. Unmodernized country homes are at an absolute premium and most properties being sold by downsizers now go to sealed bids, at least in our area. For our buyers, swirly carpets and yellow bathrooms are not a turn-off. These homes are rare as everybody wants to be a property developer these days, and buyers are getting tired of the done-up-to-sell look, which they can recognize instantly from seeing so many television shows.

There is huge demand for downsizers' homes and we can't get enough of them. If you put in a half-decent new kitchen, buyers are not going to be able to justify ripping it out, even if they don't like it. They will add up the extra cost they may be paying for a cheap off-the-peg kitchen and walk away.

I would also be careful about decluttering. Obviously it must not be a total tip, but buyers like to see graduation photos of children, for instance, as it gives them a feeling that somebody has enjoyed living there, and these vibes are picked up. If the home is too sterile, it may not seem welcoming enough.

Tracy confirms Louisa's belief that space is the thing and the bigger the kitchen the better. But she also adds that it is important to see to things like the roof, underpinning, electrics and plumbing. 'They don't have to be absolutely perfect, but a dodgy roof will certainly not get past a mortgage survey and any indication of subsidence will also make a place difficult to sell.'

Tracy also believes that the dining room is due for a comeback and that any home with a dedicated dining room is particularly desirable. So, don't automatically think that you have to knock every separate downstairs room into one huge living area before you will get a decent price for it.

Before putting your house on the market, you should get quotes and evaluations from at least five different estate agents. Louisa Fletcher says:

Somebody who has been out of the property market for 25 years or more is not going to be up to date with how estate agents have changed. A young agent is simply after commission and wants a quick sale, so may not give you the best price. If you are 78, say, you may not be used to mobile phones or everything being done over the internet, and you may prefer an older, more traditional estate agent who writes proper letters and gives you a bit of time.

Another tip is to have somebody with you when the agents call round. Many people downsizing have been widowed, for instance, and are suddenly alone. They can become intimidated by today's sales practices. Older people don't want stress, they need a buffer between themselves and a commission-hungry agent, and they have probably got massive emotional attachment to the house, especially if it was the family home for many years.

If you have a younger person with you when the agent comes to value the place, you are less likely to be hassled. I'm not saying that every older person on their own is bullied by agents wanting a quick sale, but it does happen, and valuations can be very different from agent to agent. It helps to be aware that negotiation strategies have changed, and this is where the presence of a younger person can be useful. Again, I'm not saying that agents all take advantage of older people downsizing, but it is always a slight risk.

Never forget that the main reason you are downsizing is to maximize the cash you will free up, and that this cash is absolutely necessary for your later lifestyle. So never allow yourself to be bamboozled by sales patter when you are selling your biggest financial asset, an asset you will never be able to realize again. Louisa Fletcher's website, www.propertypriceadvice.com, will give an accurate price guide in a reasonable market, a slow market and a fast-rising market.

In some cases, it may be wise to wait until the market picks up to sell at the best price, which is another reason why it is sensible to sell your home before lining up the new must-have.

Then before moving, check carefully to make sure you are not moving to a more expensive area than your present one. In some places, one-bedroom flats can cost more than three- or four-bedroom detached houses. A lot of people downsizing want to move either nearer into town, where prices are usually higher, or to a highly desirable market town or resort. If the main purpose of downsizing is to give you some cash in the bank, make sure you research your chosen areas very carefully indeed before taking the plunge. You also need to check out the council tax, as this varies from borough to borough. Council tax in the London Borough of Richmond, for instance, is more than twice as much as in the Borough of Wandsworth right next door. In fact, Wandsworth has one of the lowest council tax rates in the country and Richmond one of the highest. When living on a pension or other fixed income, the amount of council tax you have to pay can be a deal-maker or deal-breaker.

If you have made a decision to downsize, you will need to think carefully about the kind of place you want to move into, bearing in mind that you are unlikely to want to move again in a hurry. Most downsizers these days prefer immaculate lock-up-and-leave apartments to houses that may need a lot of maintenance and come with a big garden. Although gardening is a popular hobby, there is nothing worse than taking on a garden that rapidly becomes too big and a burden. When getting older, it is important to anticipate your needs over, say, the next 10 years as regards nearness of shops or public transport, neighbours, concierge or other services if moving to an apartment block, and also security issues.

In Worthing, West Sussex, the town famed for being full of old people, there is an apartment building over Marks and Spencer. These apartments always go almost before they are on the market, to older people, who can take the lift, go straight into Marks and do all their shopping for food and clothes and also have lunch there. The bus stops and coach stops are just over the road, so the extreme convenience makes up for what the apartments may lack – from the outside at least – in aesthetic appeal.

These days, you will have to make a decision about whether to downsize to a house or a flat, and there are pros and cons to each decision. Increasingly, older people are downsizing to flats, as these are cheaper, easier to maintain, friendlier and more secure than houses. As against that, you will be buying into a community, you will be interdependent on everybody else in the building, and you may have no control over how your service and maintenance charges are spent or what levies are likely to be raised. Another factor with flats is that they are usually sold leasehold, which means that you have a diminishing asset as the lease runs down.

These days, this is less of a problem than it used to be as residents now have the legal right to extend their leases for 90 years or to collectively buy the freehold from the landlord, technically known as enfranchising. But these options cost money. One retired couple I know, living in a leasehold property, were quoted £700,000 to extend their now 16-year lease by 90 years. They thought the extension was worth more like £350,000. Although they were well into their 70s at the time, they fought the freeholders over the huge cost of the lease extension and, although they were confident of winning, in fact they lost, as the court ruled the extension was in fact worth £700,000.

The upshot was that, after spending upwards of £8,000 on legal fees, the couple ended up moving to a mansion flat with a longer lease. At this time of life, you may not want such a fight on your hands, and the best advice is always to go for leasehold properties with a share of the freehold, wherever possible. This means the residents are in charge and there is no outside landlord, nor anybody making any money out of the building. This may not be possible, though, if you are moving into sheltered accommodation (see Chapter 6).

There will also be important decisions to make regarding relocating. You may want to move to just down the road, or to a completely new area. You may decide to move to the country from the town, or to the town from the country. You may want to move nearer to, or further away from, family and friends. Some downsizers decide to move nearer their adult children, while others, equally deliberately, move far, far away. My own former parents-in-law, now both dead, downsized to Minehead, Somerset, from stockbroker-belt Surrey, which put them a good four-hour car journey away from their adult children. Previously, their eldest daughter had been just round the corner and their son about half an hour away.

The matter can be, and is, endlessly debated and the only person who can decide is yourself. Never allow yourself to be browbeaten by your adult children into doing what *they* want. Only do what you want. It is your money and your life, after all.

Another essential decision to make is whether you want to buy somewhere brand new or a place that needs immediate renovation and updating. Again, you have to ask yourself whether you want to be bothered with DIY and getting workers in, or not.

There is also the question of what you will do with yourself once you have relocated, and this will have an important bearing on where you decide to go. My in-laws decided to work with charities and also went to many evening and day classes, thus filling up their time usefully. They were not particularly social people, always having friends to stay, but on the other hand they wanted a place large enough for their children and grandchildren to come and visit, especially as they had moved too far away for the families to come on a day trip.

Other downsizers move to the middle of a large town, so as to have everything to hand. If you like theatre, concerts and a busy social life, you are not likely to find it in a small village, although, having said that, my in-laws made many coach trips to London to see musicals. Just make sure you will not be cut off from your favourite activities through downsizing.

Chris and Gillean Sangster, authors of *The Downshifter's Guide to Relocation*, suggest asking yourself the following questions before making an irrevocable move:

■   If moving from a large town to a small village, will the locals welcome you?

■   Can you get the same level of service as regards doctors, dentists, taxi service, educational facilities, libraries and transport? Are there local shops still operating?

■   And, most importantly, how do you choose the correct level of downshifting? Will you want to move again in a few years?

A couple of friends, both in their 60s, sold their isolated but valuable home in three acres to move to a still-large house for four years until the wife retired from her executive job. Then they are going to move again, as they will not be able to afford their new house once the wife retires. Sensible or not? I would say not, taking into account not only the huge costs of buying and selling, but the effort of finding their next place after so short a time, especially as it took them two years to find their present place.

And here is an example of downsizing gone wrong. A friend who had lived for over 30 years in Richmond, Surrey, decided to downsize on her retirement to Torquay, in Devon. She found exactly the house she wanted, a three-bedroom townhouse in a new development, which she bought off-plan. It was cosy enough just for her but large enough to put up members of her family when they came to stay. But once she moved in she realized to her horror that all the other buyers were investors and buy-to-let purchasers, which meant she never had any real neighbours. The houses each side of her were used as holiday lets, so she had different people to cope with every two weeks or so. Although she liked Torquay itself, she was deeply disappointed with the fact that, as a single woman, she had no real neighbours and was more or less the only permanent resident in the whole development.

The moral of this story is: if buying off-plan, as many downsizers do, ask pertinent questions about the other purchasers. These days, as many as half the properties in a new development can be snapped up by buy-to-let investors. This would not suit most downsizers, who want to move into some kind of relatively permanent community rather than being isolated in an enclave of holiday and investment purchases. In Florida, homes are 'zoned' for either vacation use or residential use, to prevent this kind of thing happening. Maybe this is an idea we should try in the UK. Because of her disappointment with her retirement home, my friend is now considering another move, to Exeter, just three years after her move to a strange, new place.

But all these considerations aside, the overriding reason for most people downsizing is to free up some cash to make retirement easier, to eke out a pension when you will no longer be working, or to give money to your children to help them on the property ladder.

Having said that, some people 'upsize' when they retire. A doctor friend and her husband bought an old barn to renovate when they retired, and after about 30 years of living in their family house are suddenly embarking on house building, planning permission and dealing with builders, contractors and architects, when they are in their late 60s. Another couple in their 60s have 'upsized' to a vast house where they are constructing an underground gym and swimming pool. But these two couples have plenty of money – not the situation for the vast majority of retirees.

In any case, a lot of number-crunching is needed, bearing in mind that, with all sales and purchases of real estate, there are high entry and exit costs. It costs a lot to sell a house and a lot to buy a new property, so these figures have to be factored in when working out how much you will have left over. It is tempting to just look at the selling and purchase prices, but this is only part of the story. And don't forget stamp duty, which you have to pay every time you buy a different property.

Suppose you have a house worth £400,000 and you want to downsize to a property costing £200,000. This does not mean you will suddenly have a handy £200,000 in the bank. Estate agent fees at a typical 2 per cent plus VAT will come to £9,400, legal fees another £1,000 at least and moving costs £2,000 easily. And then there will almost certainly be things you want to buy for the new place. Curtains, carpets and white goods all inexorably add up, so that you will be lucky to come out with £170,000 for your future nest egg.

Then you have to work out the actual cost of living in the new place. What are the service and maintenance charges, if you are buying a flat? Are these likely to go up in the near future? What about transport? How much do taxis cost? Will you have to run a car in order to get in shopping?

The final aspect you will have to consider is the effect on your finances and what you want to do with the money you release from the sale of the family home. Maybe you want to help with your grandchildren's education or university costs; perhaps you want to help your own children get on to the property ladder. When I downsized in 2004 I gave my younger son, Will, £50,000 towards a deposit on his first home, making it possible for him to get on to the property ladder. I would not have been able to give him this money other than by downsizing, and when I did give it to him it was what was called a 'potentially exempt transfer' or PET, which meant that, if I lived for another seven years, there would be no IHT to pay on that amount. As it is, the taxable amount decreases by £3,000 each year until it comes down to nothing.

But because my downsizing released much more money than this, there were no real worries about Will suddenly being landed with a huge tax bill if I was killed in a road crash or something before the seven years were up. Nor did this cash gift adversely affect my standard of living. If such a cash gift does affect the standard of living, the downsizer may be on the receiving end of nasty letters from the Revenue.

In any case, you can give up to a total of £3,000 a year to your family without incurring a tax liability. If you are considering setting up a trust to benefit your children or grandchildren, be aware that trusts will not automatically eliminate an inheritance tax bill and, also, you must not compromise your own standard of living in the meantime.

Although giving money away while you are still alive will obviously reduce IHT, trusts themselves are now being taxed by the Treasury. Discretionary trusts, which means that the trustees have discretion as to how money is paid out to beneficiaries, have become popular ways to try to avoid or reduce IHT but you have to be careful. Most often, these trusts are set up to help children or grandchildren, but they will be subject to IHT if the donor dies within seven years. Also, the person giving the money – you will not have any access to it again. If you suddenly need that money for nursing care, for instance, tough: it's gone.

There are different types of trust, such as bare trusts, which are simple arrangements whereby you give money to children or grandchildren to be held until they are 18. But again, once given, it is forever out of your use. You will have to pay tax on these trusts so you will have to be very sure it is the best way of disposing of spare cash.

If you feel you cannot afford to give money away that you may need yourself in later life, you can put it into a discounted gift trust, which means you receive income for life, and avoid IHT on the lump sum paid into the trust, again as long as you live for seven years. But remember that once you put money into a trust you are no longer the legal owner of that trust, as the trust is now the owner. This is something not always grasped by those thinking about trusts. What trusts mean, in essence, is that you put that money out of your own use.

But whatever kind of trust you are interested in setting up for the purposes of reducing IHT, it must be properly set up. You will also most likely be required to have a medical check for an indication of life expectancy, as most of these trusts are insurance-based.

If you are considering downsizing in order to release cash to help your family while you are alive, rather than making them wait until you are dead, it is very much worth talking to a tax adviser or solicitor, to decide how to play it and to see whether it is actually financially advantageous to set up some kind of trust for them. When I made my last will, I decided that it was, on balance, not worth setting up trusts for my five grandchildren, then aged six down to nought. Not only would the money be out of everybody's use for too long, but the trusts themselves were expensive to set up and administer. There was, in my case, simply no point, and it was better for me to keep my money in the bank, where I could use it myself if need be, and not worry too much about IHT. But I will review the situation in a few years' time. Both laws and personal situations are liable to constant change, so beware of setting up some trust you cannot disband, if circumstances change.

A man I know, then in his 60s, gave his 30-year-old daughter a house as her advance inheritance, but a few years later he had to take it back as he was facing bankruptcy. The house was sold, and the daughter, a single woman luckily, had to move into rented accommodation.

However, for many people owning properties way above the inheritance tax threshold, the simplest way of dealing with this is simply to downsize. The money you release through downsizing will still form part of your estate, of course, although there are investment schemes available that enable you to draw down income while allowing capital to be gradually depleted. These schemes, in common with many IHT-reducing schemes, are usually linked to insurance and cost something in themselves. For any insurance-based product, there will also be commission to pay. Do not sign up to any product unless you can be absolutely certain that it is financially beneficial to you; many schemes are not, when it comes down to it.

If you can afford it, the best way of reducing your IHT liability is to downsize, give each of your children a cash sum from the proceeds, hope to live for another seven years, and leave it at that. It is always worth, as I discovered, having a useful amount of cash rather than having everything tied up in property or untouchable trusts. It makes estates easier to administer for the executors and gives you some leeway should you suddenly need cash, for instance to pay for a private operation or other healthcare. It is not always possible to get private health insurance when you are older, especially if you have a serious pre-existing condition. In any case, the level of premiums for older people is often unpayable.

Nowadays, a popular choice for downsizers is to purchase a buy-to-let property, or properties, with the money released. I did this when I first downsized, from a four-bedroom maisonette in Notting Hill to a much cheaper house in Hammersmith, and it turned out to be a very wise and profitable move. Chris and Gillean Sangster, the authors of *The Downshifter's Guide to Relocation*, reckon you need three rental properties to give you an acceptable retirement income. They also warn that it is very easy to underestimate the costs of purchasing, refurbishing and renting out these properties, and also to underestimate the sheer amount of work all this might take. You have to ask yourself whether you really want to take on such a commitment.

Never imagine that letting out properties is money for nothing, as it is often hyped up to be. There is work involved in keeping the places up to scratch, finding tenants and also complying with all the regulations necessary to rent out properties these days. Then there will be tax to pay on your profit and you will also be responsible for service charges if you are renting out an apartment.

There are two main ways of letting property: on an assured shorthold tenancy and as a holiday let. With the former, you are providing a home, a roof over somebody's head, and that person, your tenant, instantly acquires rights of occupation and cannot be easily turned out, even for non-payment of rent. Also, letting on an assured shorthold tenancy, minimum let six months, is considered unearned income, whereas renting out holiday homes is regarded as a business.

Holiday lets can bring in a good income but they are very hands-on. Also, the price the holidaymakers pay is usually an all-in amount, and you, the owner, are responsible for council tax and all utility bills, cleaning, maintenance, agents' fees, keeping up your website or other advertising vehicle, renovation and repairs. Although most holiday cottage owners employ agents, there is still a lot of work involved in maintaining such cottages to the required standards, which, I may say, are getting higher all the time.

Holiday lets have to be kept scrupulously clean and require enormous amounts of changes of linen. Before sinking any spare money into a holiday cottage, make sure you have an operating profit at the end of the day. Also, for both holiday lets and buy-to-lets, there will be capital gains tax to pay when you come to sell, at a maximum of 40 per cent.

Therefore, if considering using some of the money you free up to buy a property to rent, you have to ask yourself whether you can be bothered with all the hassle – and extra cost – that running such an enterprise inevitably entails. The equally important question to ask yourself is whether the buy-to-let or holiday cottage will actually yield more money than just putting the cash into a deposit account at the bank. Most property experts warn that you cannot rely on capital growth and must just take into account the yearly income received or receivable.

I would say that you would need to get a considerably better yield than you could obtain from the highest-level safe interest-bearing account at a bank to make it worth while renting out property when you are older or retired. The older you are, the fewer years you have to make a profit or turn a property around to produce income.

At the time of writing, I am renting out two fully owned properties, which bring in around £20,000 a year while – with any luck – increasing in value. But over the years, both have needed large sums spending on them. They should not, though, fingers crossed, need any more major cash injections for many years to come. My buy-to-lets give me options in that I could, if the worst came to the worst, always downsize still further to live in one of them.

When looking at ways to invest your money at the bank, bear in mind that any bank account or 'investment opportunity' that purports to pay well over the base rate will have risk attached; 'low risk' does not mean 'no risk' by any means. Many older people, perhaps not financially sophisticated, who have cash in the bank for the first time in their lives as a result of downsizing are sucked into investment schemes that have grand-sounding names but that put their capital at risk. The personal finance pages of daily and Sunday newspapers are full of letters from people whose 85-year-old mother has been persuaded to sign up for an investment scheme that only pays out after 15 years, for instance.

Make sure you read the small print, which often contradicts the large print. I feel that financial products should be sold the other way round, in that what is currently in the small print should actually be writ large. But then, would anybody fall for them? The advertising and sales talk is often very clever indeed, and is mainly aimed at people who do not really understand how money markets work.

Another point is that, if you do buy rental property, you will inevitably have a lot of money tied up in that property: are you likely to need to go at the capital currently tied up? In many ways, it all comes down to whether you want the simple life when you downsize, or feel up to taking on new responsibilities.

When my partner, John Sandilands, downsized, he bought a small flat to live in and two other small flats to rent out. The money from these rentals, plus the handy six-figure sum he kept in the bank, ensured a very comfortable retirement, whereas if he had gone on living in his former house he would have found himself extremely hard up. But then, he found that he liked being a landlord and was good at it. Because he had been a freelance writer all his working life he had never managed to accrue any kind of decent pension, so this solution was ideal for him.

Whatever happens, never be swayed by greed or extravagant promises. One elderly couple wanted to buy an off-plan apartment as a property pension, but were persuaded by the developer to buy 10 properties instead, putting down the same amount of money as deposits on the unbuilt properties. The idea was that they would buy to flip, that is, sell the properties at a vast profit on completion and make far more money than they ever could with modestly renting out one little flat. Well, the properties are completed now and the couple cannot sell even one, at least not at a profit. The upshot is that have lost the cash they hoped would provide their property pension. Whatever they do now, they will make a loss, which means they have downsized for no gain.

If your present estate is likely to go over the nil rate for IHT, what about making a gift of your buy-to-let properties to your children so as to reduce the value of your estate? Again, if you do this, it has to be an outright gift and not one by which you benefit as regards receiving rent or profit on resale. You would not be able to buy a property in your children's names and collect any rents. This is known as a gift with reservation and the Revenue take a dim view of it, as it seems to them you are trying to escape inheritance tax, which of course you are.

Your children would, of course, have to pay capital gains tax when they sold the buy-to-lets, but they could choose to take the income instead and benefit that way. Giving property jointly to your children only works when they all get on with each other; courts of law are littered with cases of warring children not agreeing about a deceased parent's property that has been passed down to them collectively.

When considering downsizing, it has to be worth it from every angle, and you must aim at a win–win situation.

The ideal scenario for most people would be to downsize to a comfortable home that gives them plenty of money to live on for the rest of their lives, at the same time enabling them to set up their children or grandchildren. Not everybody has enough money to achieve this happy outcome, but it is one of the best ways of making use of a property that has increased enormously in value over the years.

I would say that downsizing is only worth it when it will leave you vastly better off, cash-wise, than before.

4 Renting instead of buying

Another option you may like to consider is renting instead of buying when you decide to downsize or sell your family house.

At one time renting was considered the poor person's type of tenure, only to be resorted to if you could not afford to buy your own home. But now, thanks to the amazing success of buy-to-let in recent years, renting is becoming smart again and, increasingly, older people are deciding they might be better off renting in their later years than having responsibility for the upkeep of a house. In fact, older former homeowners are the fastest-growing group of modern renters!

For those homeowners who are asset-rich (or rich-ish) but cash-poor, renting could be the ideal answer. This is the case especially if downsizing would not actually release very much money, which is often the case. Purpose-built retirement accommodation, for instance, can also be very expensive, both to buy and for the ongoing service charges, which tend to be much higher than for ordinary apartments.

There can be many advantages to renting these days, especially as there is an increasingly wide choice of homes to rent, from simple studios or one-bedroom flats to vast country mansions, from newbuild to character properties, and from all kinds of apartments to all kinds of houses.

Renting can leave you with more money to spend, as once you have budgeted for the rent, council tax, food and utilities you have no further compulsory financial commitments. You are not responsible for the upkeep of the property and, if you take furnished lettings, you do not even have to buy any furniture or white goods. For many years, a middle-aged couple rented a fully furnished house next door to me. The husband, a banker, said that his work had taken him all round the world and he was simply tired of packing up furniture to be sent from one country to the next. He now wanted the simple life and did not want to own anything any more, even tables and chairs.

If you rent a flat on an assured shorthold tenancy, you do not even have to pay service charges as these too remain the responsibility of the landlord. In fact, present-day renting can be considered trouble-free housing, so long as you don't mind not owning somewhere, as inevitably renting a place is at least slightly less secure than owning it.

Another advantage of renting for older people is that, should you want or need to move to a nursing home later, you can do so instantly without having to sell your house first. This can be particularly important if you have too much in the way of savings or financial assets to qualify for free nursing home care. For the many financial problems older people face when having to go into long-term care, see Chapter 8.

As we all know, selling a house can take a year or more and then you may hit a bad market and not get the best price for it. Older people who are 'asset-rich, cash-poor' may decide that selling their house and living off the proceeds by renting, and having a nice lump of capital in the bank to go at, makes more financial sense than commercial equity release or downsizing to another owned house.

Another major plus of renting when you are older is that your executors do not have to worry about selling your property when you die. Although in a way this may not concern you after you are gone, the fact is that if your estate is liable for inheritance tax it has to be paid within six months of the death; otherwise punitive interest rates kick in, reducing the estate still further. And this can mean that your executors have to go for a quick sale, rather than being able to wait until the market is right to get the best price. Properties do not always sell exactly when we want them to, at the price we would like. The housing market is, at the best, capricious and there can be very good reasons for getting out of it altogether when you are older.

In fact, the more liquid assets you have in the bank, and the fewer illiquid assets, the easier your estate is to administer. Also, when renting, you don't have to worry any more about whether the value of your property is going up or down. It is simply not your concern any more and you can forget about keeping a beady eye on house prices. These days, many homeowners with quite modest properties have started to worry about inheritance tax if house prices rise too much, something they would not at one time have needed to bother about.

Because there is such a wide variety of properties available to rent, costing from £100 to £5,000-plus a week, your only concerns will be your pocket and your preference.

You can decide to rent furnished or unfurnished, have a ground-floor or penthouse flat, and live right in the middle of town, in the country or in the heart of a village. Whatever you want, there is bound to be suitable rented accommodation available. So many people are now becoming buy-to-let investors that they are snapping up all kinds of properties everywhere. And because of the great excess of supply over demand in certain areas, rents are remaining very competitive and in some cases have not gone up for years.

Renting a flat is becoming especially popular with the widowed, who often feel more comfortable in an apartment block where there are neighbours on hand than in an isolated house. Also, it can be bleak living in a house on your own when you have been used to living as one of a couple or a family.

Renting to wipe out inheritance tax

There are several ways of doing this:

■ You can give your current house to your children and rent it back from them.

■ You can sell your family home and buy a smaller home in the name(s) of your children, which you will then rent from them.

■ You can give your house to your children and move into separate rented accommodation.

■ You can sell your house to your children at a market price and move into separate rented accommodation.

All these will have the effect of cancelling out or reducing inheritance tax, but you have to be careful how you play it. As we have
seen, you cannot give something with strings attached for the
purpose of reducing IHT.

If you give your current house to your children and rent it back
from them so that you can continue to live in it, you will have to live
for another seven years before inheritance tax ceases to kick in. In
addition, in the meantime you will have to pay them the proper
rent, and not a peppercorn or nominal rent, for the scheme to work.
Otherwise, the Revenue will be on to you very quickly. You are not
allowed to pretend to give with IHT; a gift with reservation, as it is
known, is not permitted, so you would not be able to give your
house to your children in return for living in it rent-free. The only
use you would be able to make of it, if not paying rent, would be for
odd weekends or to babysit, for instance. You would not be allowed
to use it as a home for yourself as if nothing had happened.

You would also have to be careful not to fall foul of the POAT
(pre-owned assets tax), introduced in April 2006 especially to
prevent people from selling or giving a house to their children
and then moving in with them later, for nothing, as a way of
getting round IHT. The POAT charges income tax on the benefit
people are considered to have derived from assets they have
given away but that they continue to use as though they owned
them. A house worth £500,000, for example, will produce an
income tax bill of £10,000 a year at the highest (40 per cent) rate.
This tax is not payable where the proper market rent is being paid
for continued use of the property.

So what is a market rent? This is not an amount dreamed up
between you, but the rent that a commercial landlord or letting
agency would charge. If you are interested in this option, you
would have to research the current market rent by visiting some
letting agents and asking them what kind of rent they would ask
for a similar property in a similar location. For instance, if your
house is worth £500,000 you would have to pay a rent of around 5
per cent of its value, say £25,000 a year, in addition to giving your
children the house. This option, then, is only really of use to older
homeowners who have plenty of cash in the bank, or a good
income or pension, as well as owning valuable property.

If you move back into your house after seven years of living somewhere else, though, the POAT will not apply, as the seven-year rule negates it.

It is all a rather complicated way of avoiding inheritance tax, but it can work.

Case history

Shan Lloyd and her sister, Lynne, now jointly own their parents' flat in East Sheen, West London, and their elderly parents pay them rent. The elderly parents, meanwhile, are still living there.

Shan says: 'We knew anyway that the property would be left to myself and my sister when my parents died and my father, a retired bank manager, suggested putting the title deeds in our names and paying us rent so that they could stay there. They are now far too old to move, as Dad is 100 and Mum is 90.'

The idea, said Shan, was to do as much as possible to reduce inheritance tax, as the property is worth at least £400,000.

The other consideration was that, if Dad goes first, Mum could not possibly live there on her own. Although she is 10 years younger than Dad, my father gets out every day, can go to the pub, cook, and is very independent.

Mum on the other hand has a full care package from social services. She has this seven days a week, including Christmas Day. Then three days a week Mum goes to a day centre to give Dad a break. The social services people give her lunch; otherwise she has meals on wheels. Mum's carer gets her up in the morning, puts the washing in the washing machine, then at night comes back to give Mum a bath, get her ready for bed and she also gives her her tablets, which Mum has delivered from Superdrug.

The title deeds are now in our names and Dad writes us cheques for his rent. We knew this was the only way of doing it, and Dad can afford it as he has a pretty good pension from his job at the bank.

Apart from inheritance tax considerations, we also wanted to safeguard the property in case Mum has to go into a home, which she certainly would have to if Dad died first. The fact that the flat is ours means it can't be taken to pay for nursing home fees (we hope!) as Mum and Dad no longer own it, and haven't for some years.

Shan says that she and her sister had to sign a lot of documents, including an assurance that her parents would be able to continue living there. 'It was all drawn up properly with a solicitor, and not an ad hoc or informal arrangement. Although Dad is old, he is very canny and totally has all his marbles. There are no concessions for anybody, though', Shan says.

The fact that Lynne has had children and I haven't makes absolutely no difference. The property is ours in equal shares. When Mum and Dad go, the property will be sold at the current market price. It will not go to either myself or Lynne at a knockdown or nominal price. We know we will have to pay some capital gains tax, as we each have our own homes anyway, but this won't come to anything like as much as the inheritance tax. The possible care home issue for Mum was also a major factor.

As this transaction was made several years ago, they will easily bypass the seven-year rule. Plus, as Shan's father has a very good pension, his standard of living is not compromised by no longer owning property or by paying rent.

The option to give your house to your children and move into separate rented accommodation rather than buying again will also have the effect of reducing inheritance tax. This choice is known as a potentially exempt transfer.

If you do this, the seven-year rule still applies, although as you have moved into new accommodation the gift of your house to your children would not count as a gift with reservation.

If you sell your house to your children at a proper market price, after it has been valued by an estate agent (and you have the paperwork to prove it), it becomes theirs, in exactly the same way as if you sold it to anybody else. But it would have to be a proper sale, not a pretend sale, which means you would hand over the title deeds and they would henceforth own it. You would have no further claim on it at all, and you would not even have the right to claim a bedroom for your own exclusive use. If you sell your house to your children it is not a gift but a sale, although of course, if the money left over is more than the current IHT threshold, you, or your estate, will still have to pay this tax.

These are all simple ways of giving your children a nice IHT-free legacy, but you would have to have enough money left over for your own use to make any of these options legal. You are no longer allowed to live like a pauper to escape inheritance tax. If you do give your house – or a house – to your children, or sell it to them, you cannot thereby put yourself on the parish, as it were. The only way you can make these gifts or sales in later life is if your own way of life is not compromised as a result. For instance, you would not be allowed to give a house worth £300,000 to your children to escape inheritance tax and then declare yourself homeless and in need of council accommodation.

However, provided you can prove you have enough money to live at the same standard as before, giving or selling your house to your children and then renting can be a very sensible and modern idea. You would need, though, at least £250 a week available for private rented accommodation. The rent is not the end of the story, as in common with owning you still have to meet all bills. And you still have to eat.

If the option of renting attracts, you will have to think very carefully about the kind of accommodation that would suit you and, also, that would continue to suit you as you got older and possibly more infirm. For instance, would the property accommodate a wheelchair? If it is an apartment, does it have a lift? Would you be expected to maintain a garden, if you rented a country house? Does it have a bath or just a shower? Wet rooms are an excellent idea for older people who may find it difficult to climb in and out of a bath and who are nervous of slipping. Wet rooms are not common in older-style properties but they are increasingly being put into newbuilds, and are extremely popular, and not just with the elderly, either.

When renting accommodation, you cannot expect the owners to be willing to adapt it to the needs of a less mobile person, so it would have to be already what you wanted. Landlords would not be willing to install bath rails or to widen the doors for wheelchair access, for instance. And if you are interested in a place without a lift, how would you feel about humping heavy bags of shopping up several flights of stairs? There is also something else to consider about lifts: an elderly couple I know, both in their 80s and very infirm, live on the fifth floor of an apartment block. There is a lift, but sometimes careless people leave the lift doors open, or sometimes it is not working, and at such times my friends are completely marooned. They are no longer able to climb up or down stairs and they depend utterly on the lift. When they moved into their present flat, 25 years ago, they were perfectly fit and healthy.

Whenever you are making housing decisions in later life, it is important to consider carefully not just what suits you now, but what might suit you in 10 years' time, given that you are unlikely to want to make another move after one major housing upheaval.

If you already have reduced mobility or a condition such as arthritis or Parkinson's for which there is no cure, only deterioration, you might like to think about another option and that is to rent retirement or sheltered housing. Not only is this type of housing specially adapted to meet the needs of older people, but there are usually wardens or managers on duty or on call, plus panic buttons and hotlines through to local hospitals or doctors. Also, once you are in retirement housing, you are in 'the system', whereby it is easier to get access to medical or hospital care, should you need it.

Although the vast majority of retirement housing is only available to buy on a lease, or for rent to those on low incomes, you may in some instances be eligible for council or housing association retirement housing, even if you are a homeowner.

We will look at the subject of buying retirement housing in detail in Chapter 6, but it is worth saying here, while talking about renting, that if you are a homeowner you can apply directly for retirement housing to rent to any council in the country. But because there is such demand on this type of housing, you would need to be able to show a need for sheltered housing, limited financial resources when it comes to buying a retirement place of your own, plus a local connection – in other words, all three.

For instance, if you owned a terraced house in Leeds worth £90,000 and you wanted to move to the South where retirement housing costs at least £150,000, you could theoretically be considered eligible. In this situation, the proceeds from the sale of your Leeds house would not be nearly enough to buy a retirement flat in the South, where prices start at £150,000, so you would have no choice but to rent. However, you would also need to show that you had family living in the South and you wanted to be near to them. You would not be considered if you just wanted to move to another part of the country on a whim.

It has to be said, though, that if you already owned your own home, you would not go very high up on the list. The only way you would be likely to move up the list is if you could prove you had become extremely infirm and had to have sheltered accommodation and that the ordinary private rented sector could not provide for your needs.

If you rent a retirement flat from a private landlord, this will of course be on exactly the same conditions as for any other privately rented property, except that it will have been adapted for use by older people. It has to be said though that, in general, sheltered housing in the private sector is difficult to rent as there are often restrictions on sub-letting or buying to let. Most retirement housing has a communal lounge, facilities for washing and ironing, a communal garden, a warden or 'scheme manager' on duty, and often a guest suite that you can book if you want to have friends or relatives to stay. There are some extremely upmarket retirement complexes these days, so if you want to rent this type of accommodation – and you can find it – you would be extremely comfortably provided for.

The book *Choices in Retirement Housing*, published by Age Concern, makes the point that it is not always easy to find private retirement housing to rent, but advises asking the scheme manager in the area you are looking at whether any of the properties are available to rent. The local council may also have a list of such housing.

However, there is a glimmer of light opening up for older homeowners who now would like to rent rather than buy again. One enterprising man, Peter Girling, set up Girlings Retirement

Options in 1990, as the 'ultimate form of equity release'. His company buys up retirement and sheltered housing, sometimes entire developments, to rent out to older people in the private sector who have previously owned their own homes.

So, instead of downsizing and buying somewhere else, you sell your family home, pocket the proceeds and then rent a retirement apartment for the rest of your life.

Marketing manager Caroline Hull explains how it works:

> Unlike ordinary tenancies, which proceed on a six-monthly basis, once a tenant rents from us the place is theirs for life. We create an assured tenancy, which gives them security of tenure for as long as they live or have to go into a nursing home. They pay a market rent, but this is always capped in line with inflation. Although we are a business, and a very successful one, we also have a social conscience.
>
> Take a typical older person of today, a widow of 75 still living in the three-bedroom family home. It's too large for her, she can't afford to maintain it and in any case probably doesn't want the hassle of constant upkeep. On the other hand, if she downsizes, she knows she will have hardly any money left.
>
> But if she sells her home, which is worth maybe £150,000, and moves to one of our rented homes, she will free up that home for a younger family and also be able to move into a retirement complex which suits her perfectly and where help is at hand should she need it. This kind of tenant will have their pension, plus a useful sum of money from the sale of the house, as they do not have to use that capital to buy another property. All this means that our tenants can have a very comfortable retirement without remortgaging or getting back into debt.

Caroline Hull admits that many older people are resistant to renting, as they remember the bad old days when renting was considered the poor person's option and the country seemed full of rogue landlords. 'Older people often have an outdated mindset as regards renting, but once they see the advantages of renting a retirement home they like the idea. They have peace of mind and complete security of tenure, so long as they continue to pay the rent of course.'

All the properties owned by Girlings are in developments with communal areas including lounges, laundry facilities and gardens, and all have a 24-hour Careline system with a house manager on hand. Peter Girling, the founder, explains how it all started:

> I was a director of McCarthy and Stone, the best-known retirement house builders in the country, and before that I was a housing officer for Help the Aged. So I have a long background in retirement housing.
>
> We came into being during the last major downturn of the housing market, in 1988–89. There were a lot of empty McCarthy and Stone retirement homes which were not selling, and the reason for this was that people wanting to move into a retirement home could not sell their own ordinary home first, in order to free up cash to buy a retirement property.
>
> The whole thing had come to a grinding halt, so we offered these empty homes as rentals, setting up an agency to handle this. This meant that occupants could then rent out their family home for income, until such time as they could sell it.

In 1990, Peter Girling decided to form a company to buy up retirement homes as permanent rentals. 'We established a partnership with Norwich Union whereby they provide the funds and we do all the work. NU are investing in the retirement buy-to-let market, and demand is growing all the time.'

Why is this? 'Mainly because of inheritance tax', he says. 'With our scheme, which gives complete security of tenure, people can sell their family house, give some money to their children and, because they are now renting, they can budget. If they need to go into a nursing home later, they don't have to wait to sell their house.'

But renting a retirement home is not exactly the same as renting on the ordinary market. 'We take up financial, medical and personal references', says Peter Girling, 'and personally interview each prospective tenant. It is important that people move into appropriate retirement housing, and they cannot be too elderly or infirm. They must be able to live independently; otherwise they cannot be considered.'

Peter Girling believes this market will continue to grow, as people are increasingly realizing that renting can be a sensible option, and his company is now buying up whole retirement developments in order to rent them out.

There is also the fact that it is not always easy to sell a retirement home, as it cannot be sold on the open market, and there is often a premium to pay back to the developers on resale. 'The only thing that surprises me is that nobody else has picked up on the concept', says Girling. 'After all these years, we are still the only company providing this particular service.'

Actually, that is not quite true. The Grainger Trust has now entered the retirement rental market, which it believes is set to grow – fast. Peter Couch of the Grainger Trust (and also of Bridgewater Equity Release) says: 'We have bought 1,000 specialist retirement properties, some of which can be rented. We are providing an opportunity for older people to get out of property altogether and pay rent instead of buying again.'

Girlings Retirement Options now has over 10,000 retirement units being rented out. Tenants pay their rent plus service charges. With general renting, the landlord pays the service charges, but as these are always very high with retirement housing, because of the large number of services on offer, it is not practical for the landlord to cover them.

Girlings is a specialist company, set up via one man's inspiration, and the type of system it operates is not usual through the general private rented sector. This company provides a complete tenancy package and will arrange everything specifically to suit the over-55 age group.

The main way Peter Girling's company differs from other landlords is in the security of tenure it offers. This can be very important when you are older, as the usual type of tenure these days is aimed at young professionals on the move. The latest figures from the Association of Residential Letting Agents (ARLA) show that average tenancies last for 15 months. Older people renting would usually want to stay longer than that, but it may not work out.

One friend, for example, moved to a rented flat at the age of 70, after a relationship break-up. Just over a year later he was given notice to quit as his landlady, a would-be buy-to-let investor, told him she could not make it pay and had to sell the property. This meant he was looking again at the age of 71 when he had been perfectly happy in his flat. If you rent in the ordinary sector, this is always liable to happen and there is no security of tenure beyond six months – however elderly you may be.

I myself had to give notice to a 70-year-old tenant when his flat collapsed and would not be habitable again for at least four months. He had hoped to be in the flat 'in perpetuity' but there was simply no choice in the matter.

So far as renting other types of property goes, if you are considering changing from being a homeowner to a renter you will probably be out of touch with the modern rental market, especially if you have not rented yourself since your long-distant youth. Do not feel humiliated or offended if landlords, or their agents, ask for references and proof of ability to pay the rent. This is all completely standard and nothing personal to you, although if you are no longer earning you will have to provide evidence of income or capital.

You will be asked to pay a deposit of, typically, one month's rent in advance and to sign a very long, very complicated tenancy agreement. This is a legal document, a binding contract on both sides, so if you are not sure about its terms and clauses take it to a solicitor or ask somebody conversant with these agreements to sit down and go through it with you.

You will also have to sign an inventory, which lists not only the furniture and fittings that come with the property but also the condition. You as the tenant take it 'as seen', which means that you cannot complain about something later when you accepted it at the time.

Most tenancy agreements have clauses about pets, smoking and visitors, so if you are unsure about these ask before you sign the contract, not after.

A lot has been written in recent years about rogue tenants and rogue landlords but I am happy to say that both are very much in the minority. Most landlords these days bend over backwards to make sure their tenants are happy. They have to, as there is so much competition in the rental market. Most often you as the tenant will be dealing with the letting agent rather than the landlord direct, and the more upmarket your property the more likely it is you will deal only with the agent. You may not even know who the landlord is. It is also quite common these days for landlords to be large corporations rather than individuals, especially when it comes to very grand or newbuild properties.

Many agents retain 24-hour contractors for urgent repairs, so you should not have to worry about waiting weeks for a leaking tap to be fixed, for instance. If the property you are renting is fully managed, it is worth asking whether they have firms of contractors who can come out quickly to see to repairs. And the good thing is that you don't have to pay these contractors!

You will be required to set up a standing order for the rent, and the deposit will be retained until such time as you leave the property.

In the apartment building where I now live, there are at least two retired couples who are renting properties there, as they find it a simpler option than buying again. It is not an age-exclusive building but has occupants of all ages, from young children to those in their 80s. The retired renters have lovely apartments right on the seafront, which are completely looked after by other people. If they have a problem with their television aerial, the entryphone or anything else, they just call the managing agents and it is fixed right away. Well, we hope!

Renting can be a good option, but it takes a different mindset to owning and you will have to pay the rent demanded, even if you believe it is too high – maybe recalling the £2 or £3 a week you may have paid decades ago. If you do think the rent is too high, you may be able to challenge it, although the rent assessment committee (RAC) in your area will decide what the rent should be. They base their judgement on the typical market rents in the area, not on your ability to pay. It is also not unknown for the RAC to *increase* the rent on your property, if they have reason to believe it is too low.

The rent can possibly be negotiated at the beginning of the tenancy, but thereafter it is fixed and may be subject to yearly upward reviews. You can of course challenge the rise when your tenancy comes up for renewal, but may have to consider moving out. The landlord, for his or her part, will have to think about whether it is better to retain a good tenant at the same rent or risk having an empty property until somebody else can be found. Usually, annual rent rises are in line with inflation.

When renting, you will be responsible for council tax and all utilities, unless the tenancy agreement states to the contrary. Some very small rented properties, such as studios, may come inclusive of council tax and all bills except telephone bills.

There is yet another option available, and that is to sell your house and rent it back. Fullhouse Developments Ltd is just one such company offering this kind of service, and it is used mainly by older homeowners wanting to free up some cash. This is not a form of equity release, as you no longer own your home or any part of it.

This company can buy your property within seven days and no estate agents or surveyors are involved. They just buy your house as it is, in contrast with many equity release operators, who insist on certain repairs being carried out before they will release equity to you. After you have sold your house, you rent it back from the same company at the current market rent. You will have complete security of tenure – so long as you pay the rent of course – until such time as you want to leave. But because you have already sold your house, you will no longer be an owner.

Fullhouse Developments warn that, by selling your house and renting it back in this way, you will not get the full market price for your property. Instead, you will receive typically 70–85 per cent of its current market value.

Fullhouse is just one such company, and many others advertise in the backs of newspapers, often stating that the sale is completely discreet and nobody but you, the owner, need know that the place is no longer yours and that you are now renting it.

This option is much simpler than equity release, which can be a complicated operation, and makes everything easy for you, especially if you have a strong emotional attachment to your own house and cannot bear to leave. You will, of course, be able to retain all your own furniture and belongings.

Only you can decide whether you would be better off selling your house to such a company and renting it back, or selling it on the open market, usually at a higher price. As with any transaction involving large sums of money, very detailed number-crunching is required before making a decision you may later regret.

With regard to inheritance tax, what is the situation if you have divested yourself of all property ownership and have only liquid assets in the bank? Well, it is exactly the same with cash as with property, paintings or antiques, except that it will be easier for your executors to pay the tax if they do not have to have assets valued for probate and then sell them.

You can give small sums away as before, that is, up to £3,000 in any one year tax-free, or any amount provided you live for seven years after the gift is made. There is just one exception here: any gift made to a registered charity (and it must be registered to count) is free of IHT. You can only make a charitable bequest to a charity already in existence and that is listed by the Charities Commission.

But if you have decided to rent and live off the proceeds of your former home at the same time as giving sums of money away, make sure you have enough to last you out before being too generous. Never give away more than you can afford as, apart from making your life unnecessarily uncomfortable, the Revenue is likely to pounce.

Buying to let

Since 1996, buy-to-let has become a phenomenally popular type of investment, and the returns can certainly outperform other types of pension. However, if you are an older homeowner buying a property to rent out to others, you have to be aware of the various tax implications, of which there are four main ones: income tax, capital gains tax, stamp duty and inheritance tax.

You will have to pay tax on all the income you receive from rentals, although there are a number of items you can set against this, such as agents' fees, 10 per cent wear and tear, repairs and renewals, mortgage interest, and the cost of gas and electricity safety certificates, for instance.

When you buy you will have to pay stamp duty and, when you sell, capital gains tax of up to 40 per cent on the profit, and

A new foundation for your future.

Are you looking for a financially secure future? Buy-to-let offers a source of income and financial security whilst your investment continues to grow.

The Money Centre is one of the UK's leading providers of buy-to-let mortgages. With more than 15 years' experience, our award-winning team is perfectly placed to give you the expert guidance you need. From start to finish, we can ensure that your buy-to-let investment comes with maximum returns and minimum risk.

Call us now on **0800 374611** for your free consultation - and find out how we can help you to build a new future.

THE MONEY
CENTRE
Buy-to-let mortgages made easy

The Money Centre (UK) plc, Iceni Court, Norwich International Business Park, Norwich NR6 6BB
Tel: 0800 374611 www.tmcinvestor.co.uk

THE CHANGING FACE OF LANDLORDS

 Once the preserve of the monied classes ploughing their wealth into bricks and mortar, buy-to-let is now increasingly being used by young investors as an alternative to private pensions. Lynsey Sweales, marketing and PR director at The Money Centre, explains why the more mature investor no longer dominates the industry.

"Traditionally buy-to-let was the domain of the stereotypical middle-aged landlord. However, young professionals are now choosing to make a considered and long-term investment in buy-to-let property, which enables them to prepare and take control of their future."

Buy-to-let is considered a secure and flexible investment plan as well as a very lucrative business to be in, because ever since the 1900's property has doubled in value every 10.8 years. Landlords see buy-to-let as an investment that will see them safe not just for the foreseeable future, but possibly as far as retirement. Tenants pay the rent, which covers the mortgage repayments, allowing the landlord to enjoy the capital growth from the property value going up in the long term. By managing the finances on properties in a tax efficient way a landlord will never have to sell the properties.

In many cases young couples with one buy-to-let property have become landlords almost by accident – when both owned a property, but decided to live together in one and let out the other. This is similar to how buy-to-let took off in the early 1990s, when house prices suffered a sharp fall and many homeowners were faced with the decision to rent out their property rather than selling at a loss if they wanted to move house. Many took the financially-savvy option of renting out their house and the buy-to-let market was born.

There was increased confidence at the beginning of 2007 among new buy-to-let investors, heightened by record levels of total mortgage lending when it reached £24.6 billion during the month of February. This was an increase of nine per cent compared with February 2006, reflecting the continuing strength of the market and the strong desire of many people wanting to get a foot on the property ladder or move house.

The buy-to-let mortgage market is, and will continue to be driven by demand from immigrants, students and young professionals, but like any investment, there are no guarantees. However, for those who have more faith in bricks and mortar than stocks and shares, Lynsey Sweales at The Money Centre can help you minimise risks and maximise returns with ten top tips for buy-to-let investment.

1. **DO** set aside money for the unexpected – such as a void period in rent or a boiler breaking down.

2. **DO** keep an open mind about what and where to buy. Talk to as many experienced landlords as you can and learn from their mistakes and successes.

3. **DO** think carefully before buying a property with maintenance issues. Money you save buying it may be lost by it being empty while you're renovating or improving the property.

4. **DON'T** indulge your own taste in design and style of the interior or exterior of the property, as it'll restrict its appeal. Keep it neutral and safe.

5. **DO** be cautious about buying properties off-plan. You need to stick to a specific timeframe in order to maximise your return and developers may not guarantee a finish date.

6. **DO** beware of companies offering cheap conveyancing. If a few pounds saved on conveyancing means a slow service you may lose the property.

7. **DON'T** skimp by finishing your buy-to-let property with second-hand furnishings, fixtures and fittings. If they don't meet health and safety regulations you could find yourself in trouble.

8. **DO** be aware of the specialist insurance you need. Standard domestic insurance policies do not cover many of the eventualities that landlords face.

9. **DO** think carefully before leaving the management of your property to relatives or friends. Buy-to-let properties need experienced management to maintain tenant occupancy and maximise returns.

10. **DON'T** abuse the relationship you have with your tenants. Give plenty of notice before you visit and make sure maintenance problems are addressed quickly. Tenants are an essential part of your business plan and the relationship needs to be managed in a professional way.

although this tapers off the longer you have owned the property it never disappears altogether.

Any property rented out for profit will attract inheritance tax in just the same way as any other assets, although if you still own the property at your death your beneficiaries will not have to pay CGT as well as IHT.

Be careful, though, if you are considering buying a property to rent out and putting it in your children's names as, unless this is their main home, they will have to pay capital gains tax when they sell. This of course applies to any property transferred to the names of your children or other beneficiaries. You may escape inheritance tax by putting assets in your children's names, but they will still have to pay capital gains tax when they sell, whether this is property, shares, antiques or other valuables. The only exemption from capital gains tax is on the sale of your principal private residence – and each person is allowed only one of these.

An option that is becoming ever more popular is to buy two similar or identical flats, live in one and rent out the other as a pension. This will not necessarily reduce inheritance tax, but can be a neat way of financing retirement. If both properties are owned by you at death, there will not be capital gains tax to pay on the buy-to-let, so long as the property is in your name, of course, and not in the names of your children.

This, not having to pay capital gains tax as well as inheritance tax, was one of the few bonuses left to us on administering the estate of my late partner. If he had sold his buy-to-let properties before his death, he would have had to pay CGT on them. But, as they were still owned by him at death, at least we were not clobbered twice for tax.

When working out IHT liability, this is something to consider when putting properties in the names of your children or other relatives. The capital gains tax that they will have to pay when they sell the properties may work out more than the inheritance tax bill saved.

Working out the best ways to reduce or avoid tax is never easy, which is why very careful planning is needed to make sure that you really are reducing what would have to be paid out to the Treasury after your death.

Renting a property in later life instead of buying again has much to offer and should be seriously considered along with all the other possible lifestyle options available.

5 Moving and retiring abroad

The latest figures show that more than 1 million pensioners, or one in 12 Britons over 65, now live overseas. The number of 'silver flighters' is predicted to rise to one in five by 2020, according to the Institute for Public Policy Research (IPPR). The IPPR's report went on to say that the further away the location the more popular it seemed to be. Australia is the number one retirement country, with Canada coming a close second. Other popular destinations include the United States, Spain, France and Italy.

Before long, there may be hardly any older people left in the UK. And it's easy to see why they are increasingly upping and leaving. Large numbers of this age group have both money and property. In addition, they have no ties and no dependants and they are often in excellent health as well. They have most probably done a lot of travel in their younger days and are deciding to retire permanently to hotter or more congenial climes where they may have enjoyed many holidays in the past.

It sounds a wonderful idea. Why not sell up the boring old family home in the cold, damp and phenomenally expensive UK and, instead, buy a beautiful villa in sunny Spain or similar for a fraction of the price? Then you can spend the rest of your days sitting on your patio, drinking local wine and enjoying the simple life with a nice fat wodge of money in the bank.

Yes, it does sound great, and the even better news is that nowadays most of 'abroad' welcomes incomers – especially, of course, those with money. Incomers of independent means, who are not looking to earn their living in the host country but are just there to spend and boost the economy, are welcomed even more than job seekers.

Ever more of us are deciding to do it. Nearly 6 million Britons now live abroad – not all of them retirees, by any means – and every year the numbers are growing. So far as retirees are concerned, a million British people are now drawing their pensions abroad. There are currently over 200,000 British people living permanently in France, 800,000 in Spain, 600,000 in Canada and 1,300,000 in Australia.

These figures are expected to double at least within the next few years. The most popular European countries for Britons buying retirement homes are firstly Spain and France, with Italy and Portugal coming up close behind. Turkey and Cyprus are in the third rank but rapidly catching up. Malta is also extremely popular with retirees, as residents pay only 15 per cent income tax and 5 per cent inheritance tax. Also, both Cyprus and Malta have a very 'British' feel, which can appeal to retirees.

One of the most appealing reasons for retiring abroad is that, in many countries, your money goes further. In Spain, for instance, the cost of living is about 20 per cent lower than in the UK, which means your pension or lump sum left over from selling your UK house will be that much easier to eke out. In addition, you can often buy a much nicer home in France, Spain or Italy, for instance, than you would be able to do in the UK, even if you have plenty of money for a nice UK home. As I sit here writing this, looking out at leaden skies and driving wind and rain while wrapping another thick layer of wool around myself, I am opening up an email from a friend who has retired to Spain. In January, she writes: 'the sun is scorching hot and we need to pick the shady side of the house for coffees and lunch'.

Another friend has retired to France and now lives in a beautiful 17th-century manor house with a separate barn she has just converted into a gorgeous guest suite, all of which is a far cry from the tiny but expensive cottage she inhabited in rural Hampshire. Yet she sold this cottage for more than twice the purchase price of her French manor house, which means she lives very comfortably indeed on her pension plus a tidy six-figure sum left over from the sale of her UK home. My friend not only speaks fluent French but from her vantage point can easily drive to Italy, Germany or Switzerland. And if my friends in France and Spain want to visit friends or family in the UK, they just hop on a plane and are back in a few hours. Life's good, they say.

But as this book is mainly about coping with inheritance and other taxes rather than persuading you to up sticks and retire abroad for a permanent, sybaritic life in the sun, what is the situation as regards residence, inheritance, taxes and pensions?

The first thing you have to decide – as this has important repercussions – is where you want to be a tax resident. You will have to choose one country or another unless, of course, you retire to a tax haven. And you have to be very rich to be able to afford to do that.

Many countries, although not all, allow UK nationals to retire and become permanent residents there. If you are a permanent resident in, say, Spain, you are to all intents and purposes now in their tax system and have to abide by it. This includes inheritance rules, which may be different to those in the home country. Spain, in particular, is divided into regions, which are essentially autonomous, and the tax and inheritance situation in, say, Valencia may be quite different from that in Murcia. So, if you are interested in retiring abroad, you also need to check whether the region you prefer has its own tax and residency rules.

Another option is to live six months of the year in one country and six months in the home country, and this is extremely popular for retirees who can afford it. Some neighbours of mine have decided to do this. They have bought an apartment in Turkey and spend half the year there and half the year in the UK. In common with many other retirees, they have family and friends in the UK and feel they would be too cut off if they were in Turkey permanently.

Other friends who have properties abroad like the fact that they can move around and live part of the year in one country, part in another. A life of contrasts, when you have the finances and the leisure to enjoy it, can give you the best of both worlds. But beware – you will involve yourself in twice as much admin, twice as much tax planning and twice as many bills.

But even if you do decide to live half the year in one country, half in another, you will still have to elect one country as your tax domicile. This means that, if you tip over your residence by even one day, you are deemed to be tax resident in that country. As a general rule, the country where you spend more than 183 days in a tax year is deemed to be your tax domicile.

Even if you are no longer working for profit, taxes don't automatically stop when you receive your retirement pension. So long as your income exceeds the taxable amount, you will be paying taxes – somewhere. So, before you go, it's important to get a grip on all the tax ramifications regarding living abroad. The most crucial aspect is to request a state pension forecast before you go, which you can do by obtaining form BR19 from your local social security office. If you are already living abroad and want to know what your state pension income will be on entitlement, ask for form CA3638 from HM Revenue and Customs (HMRC).

As different taxation rules apply in other countries, you may want to consider the benefits of offshore banking, as this can help to reduce your tax liabilities – at a cost, of course.

You may be able to claim some social security benefits while abroad, but should also be aware that not all such benefits are transferable and some may be lost if you move abroad permanently. The leaflet 'Going abroad and social security benefits' (GL29) is helpful here. You will also want to know the situation regarding health benefits in your chosen country, as this may become crucial as you get older.

One friend was perfectly well when she first moved to France in 2002, but before long became extremely ill with multiple sclerosis. She was lucky to be able to tap into the French equivalent of the NHS but might not have been so lucky in every country. She was also lucky in that she could already speak good French.

Once you leave the UK, you will automatically be treated as a non-resident by HMRC if you subsequently visit the UK less than 183 days a year and average less than 91 days in the UK a tax year over four consecutive years. This equally applies to a spouse, civil partner or partner.

Before leaving the UK, you must inform the Revenue and get the form P85 from them. If you are non-resident in the UK you will still be liable for tax on your UK pension, although this will not be applicable if you go to a country that has a double-taxation agreement with the UK. You'll pay there instead! You can also get interest paid on your UK bank and building society accounts if you give the form R105, obtainable from HMRC, to your bank.

Many people decide to rent out their UK home rather than sell up completely, so as to have a bolt hole or pied-à-terre to return to should the foreign sojourn not work out as well as planned. In the present author's view, this is eminently sensible, in view of the fact that 20 per cent of retirees eventually do return to the UK and that most who go out as a couple will want to return if they are widowed. It takes a certain kind of stoicism to be able to live on one's own in a foreign country in later years.

If you decide to rent out your UK home, your UK letting agent will deduct tax automatically at the basic 22 per cent, although there may be relief if you are in a country with a double-taxation agreement.

If you retire to an EU country, you will be eligible for pension rises in the same way as a UK resident, but your pension may be frozen in a non-EU country such as Australia. In fact, a discriminatory state pension policy applies, as if you retire to Australia, New Zealand, Canada or South Africa your pension will be permanently frozen at the amount you were getting on leaving the UK. But retirees to the United States and EU countries have theirs increased in line with inflation, as if they were still resident in the UK. There have been many complaints about this but, at the time of writing, it is still the case that your UK pension will not go up with inflation if you retire to certain countries. So, before making a move, it's sensible to find out what will happen to your pension and how it will be paid, should you decide to emigrate.

When you move to another country permanently your situation will be somewhat anomalous, as you will be a permanent tax resident but not a national of that country. You will retain a British passport, for instance. So if you believe your assets will go over the inheritance tax limit in the UK, or you want to retain a UK home, you will need to find out what the tax and succession issues are in your chosen country. You may well have to abide by that country's legislation even if it is less favourable than that in the UK.

For instance, if you move permanently to France, you will be subject to French inheritance laws, which dictate to whom you can leave your estate. Laws of succession apply, and you may not be able to cut your children out of your will, as you are allowed to do in England and Wales, should you so choose. Once you become resident in another country, you elect to be in their system, not the one in the home country. It is not always possible to cherry-pick so that you get the best of both worlds.

Because tax and inheritance matters can be complicated when you retire abroad, it is imperative to seek advice from a tax specialist before you leave – not once you are there.

Selling up completely

If you are intending to sell up completely and not retain a pied-à-terre in the home country, you will then become, to all intents and purposes, a permanent resident of your chosen country, and you will lose any tax benefits obtaining in your native country.

Generally speaking, as a UK national you have the right to live freely in any European Economic Area country. As there are now 27 countries that are full members of the EU, this gives plenty of options, although all these countries retain much of their separate identity and have different tax, retirement and inheritance laws.

Spain

Here is a brief guide to the situation in Spain, by far the most popular European retirement country for Britons. Before deciding whether to reside permanently in Spain, it is a good idea to seek advice from a financial adviser qualified to give cross-border advice, as tax and financial matters can be complicated.

In general, anybody spending 183 or more days in Spain during the tax year is deemed by the authorities to be a tax resident and is liable to pay Spanish tax. If you are considered a tax resident in Spain you will be liable for Spanish tax on all your assets worldwide, including those in the UK, if any.

Although in theory you may also be liable for UK tax, there is in operation a double-taxation treaty, which ensures you do not pay tax twice. But if you are not technically resident, which means you are spending less than 183 days in Spain each tax year, you will still be liable to pay Spanish tax on income arising in Spain, such as for renting out property. Even non-residents have to pay a small amount of annual tax if they own property in Spain.

Wealth tax, as it is known, is calculated on the sum of your assets held in Spain and is imposed on both residents and non-residents. A non-resident pays wealth tax (not the same as inheritance tax) at the same rate as a resident, the difference being that, whereas a non-resident only has to declare Spanish assets, a resident must pay this tax on all assets worldwide. However, the upper amount of this tax is 2.5 per cent – and that's on assets worth over 10.5 million euros.

If you are moving to Spain permanently, it is worth finding out about offshore trusts, whereby you give your assets to 'trustees' located in a low-tax-regime country or area, after which your assets are no longer treated as yours for tax purposes. Once your assets are put into trust, you will only be able to receive the income on those assets and not touch the assets themselves. Such trusts can help your beneficiaries to avoid inheritance tax but, warns Guy Hobbs, author of *Retiring to Spain*, they must be set up to comply precisely with Spanish law, bearing in mind that Spain, unlike the UK, is a civil law country with a written constitution.

Pension matters

If you are in receipt of a UK pension, you should make arrangements to have this paid directly into your Spanish account before you leave the UK. There is now a well-trodden path to enable you to do this without complications. Your pension will continue to rise in accordance with UK inflation, although pension credit is not payable outside the UK. Most people who retire to Spain, though, will have some financial assets and, therefore, are unlikely to be in need of pension credit.

However, if you receive a public sector pension, this is paid into your account after UK tax has been deducted. It will form part of the double-taxation treaty agreement, though, so you should declare it on your Spanish tax return as taxed income.

If you receive a private pension, this will be paid according to the strictures of the UK company. Some company pensions can only be paid into a UK account, which means you will have to set up a standing order to have the money paid into your Spanish account. And all of these transactions will incur bank charges. Because of this, it will pay to shop around to get the best deal, as in some cases you will be paying twice – once for the transfer and then commission from the Spanish bank.

If you are not of retirement age but do not intend to work for money on arriving in Spain, you should continue paying National Insurance contributions in order to qualify for a UK state pension on reaching retirement age. You will also be able to have a retirement pension forecast, and this is very advisable, as it will enable you to know how much money you will be getting each month.

Some financial benefits from the UK will still be available to you in Spain. These include bereavement allowance and widowed parents' allowance. However, you will no longer be entitled to receive disability living allowance, income support, pension credit, attendance allowance and carer's allowance. The winter fuel allowance, though, will continue to be paid, even though in Spain you will very probably not need it!

All this, though, could mean that your total pension is substantially reduced on your retirement to Spain, so you will have to make sure you can still afford to live there, both now and later, if you should become disabled or infirm.

You can continue to contribute to a private pension scheme once resident in Spain, or you could consider taking out a Spanish pension plan.

So far as personal taxation goes, you will need a tax reference number for foreign residents and also for property-owning non-residents. You will probably find you are paying about the same amount of tax in Spain as you would in the UK, and you will not be entitled to receive any special tax relief as a foreigner.

Making a will

It is essential for anybody buying property in Spain, whether or not they intend to become permanent residents, to make a

Spanish will. This avoids the time-consuming procedure of waiting for probate in the home country. Most people resident in Spain make two wills, one for disposal of their Spanish assets and another to deal with any UK assets. Experts say you should not try to combine the two, but keep them very separate, while making sure the two wills are in harmony with each other.

Although Spanish inheritance laws, in common with French ones, are more restrictive than those in the UK as regards who should inherit, foreigners are not subject to the rules of 'compulsory heirs' and can leave their assets to whom they please.

Do be aware though that you will be liable for Spanish inheritance tax, known as succession tax, although this is only high when property or other assets are left to complete strangers rather than close relatives. Inheritance tax in Spain can kick in at a rate as high as 82 per cent on inherited wealth, which is paid by the person(s) inheriting rather than on the estate of the deceased.

If you are, or have become, a permanent resident in Spain, then all your assets worldwide will be subject to succession tax on your death, but as a non-resident you would only be liable on your Spanish assets. If the beneficiary is a resident of a country with a double-taxation agreement, he or she would not be taxed twice.

Also be aware that if you are a joint owner of a Spanish property there is no automatic inheritance by other owners and, even if the property is left to a relative, there will be a transfer tax payable. There is, though, a sliding scale of payments according to consanguinity, and near relatives are entitled to receive a proportion of the estate tax-free.

One dodge here, at least as regards Spain, is that you can register a newly purchased property in the name of the beneficiary, thus ensuring minimal taxes. The tax payment is calculated on the degree of kinship between the deceased and the person inheriting, and relief is available on family homes if the property remains in the ownership of the recipient for at least 10 years after the original owner's death.

Because Spanish succession tax can be extremely complicated, it is essential to seek the advice of a financial adviser fully conversant with these laws. Bear in mind that most EU countries have inheritance taxes and laws that are very different from those in the UK.

Other tax matters

Non-residents will have to pay capital gains tax (CGT) at 35 per cent when they sell their Spanish property, whereas residents can roll over CGT to a new property. The CGT in Spain discriminates against non-residents, and this may influence your decision if you believe you might sell your existing property and buy another.

Healthcare

Either way, if you are of UK pensionable age, you must obtain the form E121 from the UK Department for Work and Pensions if you have reached pensionable age. This entitles you to free healthcare on the Spanish equivalent of the NHS. If you have not reached UK pensionable age, but do not intend to work for money in Spain, you have to get the E106, which entitles you to free healthcare for a certain length of time.

A letter in the *Guardian* on 3 February 2007 makes the point that, contrary to popular belief, not all Brits living in Spain are 'mono-lingual Costa cockneys or pensioners fixated on the local healthcare facilities'. 'A large proportion of us', writes Chris Towers from Madrid, 'are fully integrated, participate in and contribute to western Europe's most dynamic economy beyond merely inflating the local housing bubble'.

British people – and indeed other Europeans – have become extremely important to the Spanish economy, and the country does as much as it can to welcome Brits and make life easy for them there. But just recently there have been some horrific tales of people who took early retirement to settle in Spain and then became extremely ill, with the result that they had to return to Britain to take advantage of free healthcare. But these people did not find it easy to sell their Spanish property and buy some-where new in the UK. If you are below pensionable age when you retire to Spain you are not automatically entitled to free healthcare in Spain.

Although nobody can accurately predict the future, healthcare provision in your chosen country is something to consider very carefully when you are older.

France

Much of the advice pertaining to Spain is also applicable in France, as both countries are subject to Napoleonic laws that determine inheritance and succession. Any property held directly in France is subject to inheritance tax although, just to complicate matters further, if the property is held through an SCI (Société Civile Immobilière) – a transparent company that counts as a separate legal entity – the value of your assets can be reduced. Financial experts warn, though, that an SCI is complicated to set up and also that there are severe penalties for tax avoidance.

It is true that French-approved life insurance policies can reduce tax, although these policies are expensive in themselves to set up.

The big fear for most people thinking about retiring to France is that it is a land of high taxes. The top rate is 49 per cent, but tax advisers say that a couple with an annual joint income of 70,000 euros or less would be better off retiring to France.

If you become a French resident, you will be taxed on your worldwide income, as in Spain, and any pension drawn out of the UK must be declared in France.

You will have to pay French inheritance tax on assets coming to more than £504,000 (in 2007), and also abide by French inheritance laws, which govern who inherits your assets, whether property or liquid assets. But French succession tax is levied at 20 per cent over the nil-rate band, as opposed to 40 per cent in the UK, so your heirs might be better off inheriting your French property. It is the case though, again as in Spain, that the beneficiaries rather than the estate are liable to pay the tax.

At the time of writing, there is no succession tax payable by each beneficiary bequeathed 152,000 euros or less.

UK buyers now account for over 40 per cent of international sales in France and, if you become a tax resident, there is no capital gains tax payable on the sale of your French home. By contrast, you will be liable if you have a holiday or investment property there.

Italy

Italy is one of those countries that does not have inheritance tax, along with Cyprus, Gibraltar, Malta (well, it is very low in Malta) and Portugal. This may well influence your decision if you are not sure which country to pick for the best.

There are two degrees of residency in Italy. If you want to spend more than 90 days there you must obtain a residency permit from the local police station. You will also have to get a fiscal code number from the local tax office, as this is needed for many formal agreements from property leases to mobile phone contracts.

Non-EU countries

It is more complicated – even more complicated – to retire to a non-EU country, and in some cases you cannot do it at all. You are only allowed to stay in the United States for six months at a time, and cannot retire permanently there, however much you may want to   unless you have very large sums of money to put at the United States' disposal, that is.

You are allowed, as a UK national, to retire to Australia, Canada and New Zealand, and these countries are very popular indeed with retirees.

Australia and New Zealand

Australia is, as we have seen, the most popular country of all for retirees, and Australia has a special investor retirement visa, initially available for four years, which is precisely tailored to those who just want to enjoy themselves down under.

There are, though, strict requirements that have to be fulfilled before this type of visa can be issued. First, you must be over 55 and have no dependants, although you can be a couple, married, in a civil partnership or in a long-standing relationship. In addition, you must be financially self-supporting and able to show you have sufficient assets not to be a burden on the health or social security system. Financial requirements differ from state to state, but a minimum would be Aus$500,000. You must be able to show a minimum income stream, from investments, royalties (if a writer or artist) or pensions. You will also have to have private health insurance and, finally, you will have to show you are of good character.

These visas run for an initial four years, after which they can be renewed if you fulfil exactly the same requirements. It is made plain that these visas do not lead to permanent residency, nor do they confer Australian citizenship, although in most cases renewal of the visa is a formality once you have satisfied the initial four years.

So far as working is concerned, you are allowed to work up to 20 hours a week, although you are definitely not on a work visa. When my friends, writers Julia and Derek Parker, retired to Australia they had to fulfil an unusual requirement as regards work. They were allowed to write for British publishers but not Australian publishers in case they took work away from a native writer. There was no problem, however, about one of their books being sold to an Australian publisher after it had been published in the UK.

South Africa

You will be welcome to retire to South Africa but will need to have a joint pension (for a couple) of at least £1,450 a month to qualify for residency. One possible drawback is that your state pension will be frozen when you emigrate and the amount you receive when you enter South Africa will never ever rise – unless the law changes, of course. But such a change is not, at the time of writing, even the merest glimmer on the horizon. In order to be allowed to retire in South Africa, you must be able to demonstrate either a lifelong pension or adequate income from a combination of assets. Otherwise, you will not be allowed to retire there. The government emphatically does not want foreign retirees being a drain on the economy, and to become a permanent resident you must be granted a permanent residence permit. The South African embassy has all visa details you need.

Canada

Much of Canada is stunningly beautiful and of course, for British people, does not feel that 'foreign', even though it is so far away. It is currently the fourth most popular country to retire to, after Spain, Australia and France.

But in some ways it can be tricky to retire to Canada. As with all other countries, Canada has complicated tax and residency arrangements, which have to be carefully considered before you impulsively buy a beautiful ski chalet or romantic log cabin on the edge of one of the lakes.

Canada, unlike Australia, does not have a special retirement visa, which could make emigrating for retirement purposes difficult. If you already have family over there, then of course your passage is considerably eased. One friend living and working in Canada 'imported' his elderly father from the Midlands to live with him and his family, and that was straight-forward enough. But ideally you would need to work for a few years in Canada before retiring there. In any case, it is essential to consult a Canadian immigration expert to see where you stand.

As with every other country – maybe everything in life – there are practical pros and cons to retiring to Canada. One of the worst aspects is that, on retirement, your UK state pension is frozen. This is the case with most former Crown colonies and has some-thing to do with agreements made years ago with new govern-ments when they were granted independence. If you retire to an EU country, by contrast, your UK state pension will rise in line with inflation.

Of course, private pensions are unaffected by this rule, but there is yet another complication. The Canadian tax system does not recognize the UK entitlement to take 25 per cent of your pension out in tax-free cash. The way round this, if you want to do it, is to take out this money and start drawing your pension before you leave the UK. Your pension will be taxed at the rate payable in Canada, not the UK, once you have retired there permanently.

These are two complications, but it gets worse. Canada has two distinct layers of income tax, the provincial tax for each of the 12 provinces, and the federal tax. To make matters even more complicated, each province has its own tax rate. Just to give an example: suppose you have an annual income of £65,000, you would pay tax at 39 per cent in Alberta, but 46.4 per cent in Toronto. Canada is emphatically not a low-tax country and we will see why in a minute.

You will become liable for income tax after spending 183 days in Canada in any calendar year. These days do not have to be consecutive. In this regard, Canada is in line with all other countries.

Now for some upsides. The good news is that inheritance tax does not exist in Canada, and capital gains tax is also much lower than in the UK. But if you are emigrating to Canada to escape UK inheritance tax, you will have to wait five years before HMRC forgets about you. In other words, if you die three years after emigrating, the UK inheritance tax laws still apply.

Capital gains tax in Canada ranges from 7.5 per cent to 23 per cent – vastly lower than the UK rate of 40 per cent, which makes Canada an ideal country for those with considerable capital gains tax liability. So if you own a number of buy-to-let properties, holiday cottages or stocks and shares, for instance, make sure you retire to Canada to take full advantage of the vastly lower rates. When you retire to Canada, your assets will be revalued for CGT purposes, as you will now be tax resident there.

The other two main advantages of retiring to Canada are that property is considerably cheaper than in the UK, and the healthcare, by all accounts, is magnificent and completely free. There is no private healthcare system as such in Canada but again, if you are considering emigrating, you will need to find out whether you are covered for every health eventuality. Also, gaining access to all the health systems may take time, so the expert advice is to have health insurance at least for the first few years of your residency there.

It will be essential for you to make a new will as soon as possible, as your UK one will no longer be valid. Financial experts also advise using a specialist currency company to organize your currency and take advantage of currency fluctuations. This of course applies to any country where you might considering settling.

The United States

To all intents and purposes, Florida is the only state popular with British retirees. Eleven hundred Americans a day retire to Florida, and this would be at least equalled by the number of Brits if only it were easy for them to retire to Florida.

Briefly, the situation is this: there is no retirement visa obtainable as such, and those wishing to retire to Florida have a choice of applying for a B2 visa or an EB-5 visa.

The B2 is simplest, but only allows you to be in Florida for six months of the year. This means that you would have to have a place in the UK, or other EU country, to keep going back to.

Your other option, the EB-5 visa, grants permanent residence, but at a very high price. In order to be eligible, you have to invest around $500,000 (about £267,000, depending on exchange rates) in a US business. Your investment has to create employment, and can be in commercial real estate, farmland or another similar area. The money has to be held in an approved investment project for two years, during which time you would get around 6 per cent yield. The money can be refunded to you after two years, by which time you would be able to have the coveted Green Card, which enables you to stay in Florida permanently. The investment project does not have to be in Florida – one couple who retired in this way invested the money in commercial real estate in Seattle.

As with any investment, though, there cannot be an absolute guarantee that you will get your entire stake back or that your investment will make money in the meantime so that you end up richer than before. All investments carry some risk, although as the money has to be invested in a government-approved scheme it is not a high risk.

The visa processing takes typically 9–12 months, and requires an exhaustive interview at the US embassy in either London or

Dublin, after which time a conditional Green Card is issued if you are approved. This is at the moment the only way for retirees to enter the US permanently and means that a lot of your money is tied up for quite a long time.

However, those who have managed it say that Florida retirement villages are absolutely wonderful and nothing like those in the UK. Instead of walking along a cold windy beach, they say, you can look at sparkling seas, eat outside, swim in your pool, play golf all year round at the championship-quality golf course attached to the retirement village and generally have a wonderful time.

So far as inheritance goes, in Florida you are allowed to leave your money to whomever you choose. There are no automatic rights of succession, as in some European countries, where you are required to leave money to your children, not just your spouse.

If you are a permanent resident in Florida, you will pay estate tax according to US laws, and if you own property but are not a permanent resident you can face a hefty tax on the value of your estate at the time of your death. There is only a partial exemption for transfers between husband and wife, not total exemption as in the UK. Just make sure, if you are not a permanent resident in the United States, that your estate is not taxed twice.

Again, it is essential to discuss it all very carefully with a tax adviser conversant with the systems in both countries before you go. Very many people buy property in Florida without understanding their tax liability – and then find themselves being tied up in extremely expensive knots. If you are not a permanent resident in Florida, the amount of US estate duty you pay can be deducted from liability to IHT in the home country.

If you are a permanent resident, exemptions from estate duty are lower than for non-residents. In fact, you pay nothing on the first $2 million of your estate, as opposed to liability after $65,000 for non-residents. As in the UK, assets of the estate cannot be disposed of until inheritance tax is paid.

Capital gains tax is payable on the sale of any asset, including property, when you sell. Non-US residents have to pay CGT on any sales in the United States where there is a gain, usually at a standard 30 per cent. Non-residents can, though, choose to pay

CGT at a lower rate. This would also involve paying CGT on their worldwide assets.

If you are considering buying property in Florida and retiring there, whether permanently or as a non-resident, it is essential to sort out all the tax and inheritance liabilities that may concern you and make sure you understand the implications of each option before buying anywhere.

If I were going to retire to Florida, I would first of all contact the US embassy, tell them that I wanted to retire there permanently, and hammer out all the options, including the payment of $500,000 to secure the EB-5 visa. Then I would ask about inheritance tax, capital gains tax, healthcare (expensive!) and any taxes I might have to pay to the Internal Revenue Service. I would also want to know that my $500,000 would be safely invested with a government-approved company and that I would be sure to get interest plus the capital back after the requisite time. I would also want reassurance that I would be granted a Green Card and would not be kicked out of the country after a couple of years.

Those who have permanently retired to Florida admit that going through the immigration process is a horrendous business – but say it is well worth it once you are there. Bear in mind also that if you have a pre-existing serious health condition you may not find it easy to get health insurance.

When property changes hands, the IRS takes a percentage, which you have to work hard to get back.

You do not have to live in a retirement village if you retire to Florida, but can choose any type of home in this vast state the size of Europe.

Tax matters in general

First of all, you must contact HMRC and get a form P85 to obtain any tax refunds to which you may be entitled, and they will work out whether you will become a non-resident. You may need to complete a tax return form after you leave the UK.

If you earn money overseas, you will not pay UK tax on this income once you become non-resident. But you will be liable for UK tax on your UK pensions, including your state pension, if your total income exceeds the nil-rate band for tax. This may not be the case if the country to which you are moving has a double-taxation agreement with the UK.

You will usually pay UK tax on bank and building society interest accounts but, if you are not ordinarily resident, you can get interest without tax deducted by giving form R105 to your bank. UK tax is still due on any other UK investment income, although again you can get relief or exemption if the country where you now live has a double-taxation agreement.

The whole thing is complicated and you may want to work out whether you will be better or worse off tax-wise before deciding whether to go. It has to be said that HMRC is clamping down hard on anybody who tries to evade tax – and you cannot just move to another country and try to vanish from the UK tax system.

Moving to a tax haven

There are a number of countries in the world where no tax is paid. Great – but what does this mean in fact? Retirement expert Rosemary Brown, writing in *Saga* magazine, warned: 'There is no corner of the globe which is left untaxed, and many so-called tax havens fail to live up to their reputation.'

If you want to retire to a tax haven – and who wouldn't want to retire to somewhere you never have to pay any tax? – you may find that stringent rules and conditions are imposed on foreigners. For instance, you may have to produce documentary evidence of a very high annual income – a rock star or tycoon income and not something modest and ordinary – or you might be required to deposit a large sum with the government in case you have to be repatriated. In general terms, it is not possible to retire to a tax haven unless you are already very, very rich.

As we have seen before, those who are already extremely rich can usually escape all kinds of taxes that are unavoidable by ordinary people. It may be possible, if you are very clever, to avoid paying taxes by having three retirement homes: one in the UK, one in the South of France and the third in the United States, for instance. But then you would have to have a very high annual income to be able to afford three retirement homes in the first place.

Domicile versus residency

Although the terms are often used interchangeably, there is a technical difference between being 'resident' and being 'domiciled'. In general terms, you are considered to be domiciled in the country where you have your permanent residence. You may be resident in more than one country but can only be domiciled in one country at a time. If you are resident abroad and intend to spend the rest of your days in that country, it may be advisable to change your domicile.

In any case, it is essential to take up-to-date tax advice, as tax rules in all countries are liable to sudden and frequent change.

Inheritance tax

Retiring or moving abroad permanently does not necessarily mean you will escape paying UK inheritance tax. In general terms, you will still be liable if you were not domiciled overseas for all of the last three years before death.

You may escape, though, if you were resident overseas for more than three tax years in your final 20 years of life and all of your assets are overseas anyway. But if you were resident overseas without being domiciled, you (or your estate) will still be responsible for paying IHT at UK rates.

In general, you will be treated as non-resident in the UK for tax purposes if you can show that you left the UK to live abroad permanently and that your visits back to the UK are less than 183 days in a tax year. The same will apply to your spouse, civil partner or partner.

But, as it can be complicated, it is worth speaking to a specialist tax adviser – your local branch of HMRC should have somebody who knows all about it – before you make any irrevocable decisions about retiring abroad.

So, to sum up, if you are considering retiring abroad, you need to find out your tax position on pensions and income, capital gains tax, succession laws and inheritance tax, just to make sure you do not get any nasty unexpected shocks.

6 Sheltered and retirement housing

Sheltered, or retirement, housing is one of the fastest-growing housing sectors all over the world. It is in increasing demand, as people are living ever longer and, although such housing appears to be built at a furious rate, seemingly filling in every little gap in every town and village, there is still nowhere near enough such housing to meet the demand. Just 13 per cent of all retired people in the UK live in specially built retirement housing, or assisted living, as it is increasingly coming to be known.

But demand aside, what are the pros and cons of this type of housing? There are two radically opposing views. One is that it is an overwhelmingly good idea, as this type of housing is specially adapted to the needs of older people, and the other view is that it's a crying shame to shovel all elderly people into gated ghettos where they only ever see other elderly people.

Another argument against sheltered housing is that values of such properties often go down, rather than up. Here is a typical scenario. When a new development is built, most buyers will be in their late 60s or early 70s. Mostly, these buyers will not want to move again, so stay there either until they die or until they have to move into a nursing home. The result is that, 10 years on, this same development will be peopled with occupants who are all in their 80s, getting increasingly frail, deaf and immobile. This means that a recently retired 68-year-old, say, will not want to move into a development consisting only of extremely elderly people.

As the original buyers become ever older and more frail, the fact that the 'young old' do not want to move into such a development can make the units difficult to sell when an original owner dies or has to go into a nursing home. Also, a 10-year-old development may not look as nice and new as a recently completed one.

The retirement home sector is tricky and can be difficult to get right, although there is undoubtedly much to be said for moving into a development that has been built specifically with older people in mind. There is the other factor that there are no children, usually no noise and very little anti-social behaviour. Although one does hear of older people being given ASBOs, this is not a common occurrence. As all, or at least most of, the occupiers will be retired people, they have more time to develop a sense of community, to serve on committees and to generally be friendly and helpful. Moving to a retirement home can also be a good idea for older people now on their own, as they are less likely to be lonely and ignored than when in ordinary housing.

My former mother-in-law, who ended her days in sheltered housing, used to complain that everybody in her communal lounge was deaf and that she never saw anybody under 80. On the other hand, when she became ill and pressed the Careline button, a medical team arrived instantly. So, in spite of all her complaints, sheltered housing was really the answer for her.

If you prefer to remain in your own home, this can perhaps be adapted to your needs as you become more elderly, but home-owners should be aware that these adaptations can make the house lose value. Such devices as grab rails on baths, panic buttons, switches at waist level and ramps for wheelchairs are all very useful adaptations for older people but can put younger buyers off. This is especially the case if it would be expensive to dismantle a walk-in bath, for instance, and install a normal bath instead.

There are, as with anything else in life, degrees of sheltered housing. You can go very up market and pay £500,000-plus for a very smart sheltered apartment with colour coordinated communal areas, or you can go for a very small studio apartment with room only for a small single bed in the living room. Also, not all age-exclusive apartments are designated 'retirement' complexes. Although all developments aimed at the older market will have at least some adaptations, such as specially wide doors for wheelchairs, not all will have facilities such as a scheme manager, communal lounge, or laundry or Careline facilities.

As a general rule, though, retirement apartments are rather small and, for many elderly people, this will be their very first experience of communal living, of having their own quarters in a place that does not entirely belong to them. For those who have previously lived in a freehold house, this sort of housing can seem just one step away from a nursing home, for although you have your own front door and can fill the apartment with your own furniture, so long as it will fit in, of course, you will inevitably have to adapt to community living, at least to some extent. This type of housing may not be suitable for grumpy old men – or grumpy old women.

If you are interested in sheltered housing, the first thing to find out is whether you can afford it, as there are ongoing compulsory costs, and these do not stop with the purchase price. If you have previously lived in a freehold house, it may come as a shock to realize that you will have to pay service charges to the freehold company.

First, a few statistics. There are currently around 9 million people of pensionable age in England, of whom 90 per cent live in general housing. Around 13 per cent of those aged 80–84 live in retirement housing, and 19 per cent of those aged 85-plus. There are currently 105,000 retirement properties in the UK, although more are being built all the time. One advantage about this type of housing is that, because it usually consists of flats rather than separate houses, developments can be built in small spaces on brownfield sites.

Retirement housing, as opposed to merely age-exclusive housing, is usually built in a development of 15–60 units, which are usually one- or two-bedroom flats, although there may be some bungalows in large developments. All developments have communal facilities such as a lounge, laundry and guest room and there will be a scheme manager employed by the management organization whose job it is to look after the development, although this person will not provide personal care or help with shopping, for instance. All such housing has emergency alarms, which are connected to a monitoring centre monitored round the clock. It is this aspect, more than any other, which most endears older people to retirement housing.

Some developments will also have restaurants that provide lunches and dinners, and a small extra charge is made for this optional extra, as all flats have cooking facilities. You will be responsible for organizing cleaning in your own flat, although you will have no maintenance or repair worries. The management organization in charge will see to all repairs and these will normally be met out of the service charge. Usually, the management company will have to approve a buyer, to make sure the 'wrong' sort of people don't move into the development.

The first step would be to contact the Elderly Accommodation Council (EAC). This gives free advice to older people to enable them to make sensible decisions about housing in later life. AIMS (Advice, Information and Mediation Service) is a specialist concern run by the charity Age Concern, which gives information and advice specifically on retirement housing.

The average age at which people move into retirement housing is 72 and the majority of residents will be in their 80s.

Churchill Retirement Living, an offshoot of McCarthy and Stone, perhaps the best-known retirement housing company, now offer seminars to make it easy for older people to consider downsizing. They also offer a home exchange service whereby they will arrange two independent valuations of your existing property. You are then presented with a home exchange offer, and your solicitor can proceed with exchange of contracts and completion. Note that this offer may not represent the best market price for your existing home, as it is a commercial service.

The seminars will also help you to get rid of perhaps 60 years of accumulated clutter by arranging garage sales. Churchill can put you in touch with Moving Angels, a pre- and post-move and small repairs service where everything is packed and unpacked and put into place, and any minor repairs or electrical work can be carried out so that you can start living in your retirement apartment right away.

Most retirement developments are situated on small sites, which are usually in urban locations. Very often, they are right on the main high street in easy reach of transport and shops.

But another solution is becoming popular, and this is the concept of retirement villages. These have already proved themselves in Florida and Spain, and are now starting to catch on in the UK. These villages are rather different from ordinary retirement developments in that they are not mixed in with standard housing. Instead, a whole 'village of the damned' (no, not really!) is constructed, with everything on hand.

Typically, a 'retirement village' will be built around a substantial existing period property. This 'big house' provides administrative offices and leisure facilities, and new flats and houses are built in the often extensive grounds of this former stately home. The 'village' will also have restaurants, bars, shops, a library, an auditorium, a swimming pool, tennis courts and other leisure facilities such as bridge and chess clubs, so that it will provide more or less a self-contained community.

John Gooding, chief executive of Retirement Villages, explains how these communities work: 'We are mainly selling lifestyle choices', he says.

> The inhabitants decide what they want and we try to accommodate their wishes. The idea is that our residents will be able to have a good time whatever their interests and it is our job to facilitate the services required. At the same time, residents are buying solid bricks and mortar, so the villages work financially for them, as well. The homes can be sold on to other qualifying people and, as such, represent an investment as well as a great way to spend your retirement years.
>
> As these villages are being built to a high standard, annual capital growth of around 8 per cent is expected and although occupants have to be over 50, or over 60 in some villages, there is nothing to prevent younger people from buying such a residence for an elderly relative.
>
> Many of our residents have said that moving to a retirement village takes 10 years off them.

Overwhelmingly, the retirement village offers security, and the fact that most residents will be at or near retirement means there is no 'rowdy element', as can arise in mixed-age communities. One such village, St George's, near Brighton, East Sussex, is being built around an Augustinian religious community. The sisters in the community are on hand to provide healthcare. This project is due to be completed in 2009, with 235 residential units.

Another retirement company, Audley, takes important listed buildings and turns them into retirement villages. Nick Sanderson, the CEO, said: 'There are three distinct demographics: the 55- to 75-year-olds, active over-75s and, finally, frail older people. Integrated communities that can cater for all three groups in the one development are the future for retirement housing, and retirement providers must offer adaptability for residents as their needs change.' Audley says it offers as much or as little help as residents require. A similar scheme, Historic House Retirement Homes Ltd (HHRH) offers individual apartments surrounding a grand country house where nursing care can be offered if needed later.

HHRH was the brainchild of Nigel and Simon Whalley, who inherited a nursing home business from their parents. They decided to construct individual apartments around the main house and offer 'assisted living' for residents who might need it.

The individual apartments are occupied under a lifetime licence. You pay a deposit to secure this licence, which is returnable when you leave. Although this type of tenure cannot be considered an investment, in some cases the value may go up and residents can benefit from this increase when their deposits are returned. In addition you pay a service charge of between £1,500 and £3,000 a month, so you do have to be quite well-heeled to afford this luxurious type of retirement living.

In return for the service charge, residents get a weekly laundry service for sheets and towels, twice-weekly house cleaning and monthly window cleaning, maintenance and repairs, lunches, a minibus for shopping and other outside trips, utilities and council tax paid. So – you get quite a lot back in return for your monthly outlay. In addition, all the individual apartments and cottages have cooking facilities if you prefer to eat alone.

Lifetime Homes are overseen by the Joseph Rowntree Foundation, and are rather different from the above in that they are a charitable foundation, and the Joseph Rowntree Housing Trust is a registered social landlord. Lifetime Homes are mainly newbuild and are specially adapted for older and disabled people.

A report commissioned by the Joseph Rowntree Foundation in 2006, entitled *Making the Case for Retirement Villages* and written by

Karen Croucher of York University, makes the following points. Older people are increasingly seeing retirement villages as positive choices, as they combine independence with security. Retirement villages can offer facilities, such as nursing care services, which would not be viable in smaller developments. Retirement villages also promote health and well-being in older people and they can address the current and future needs of older people as well as releasing significant numbers of under-occupied properties for use by younger people. Retirement villages, the report concluded, are a relatively new development in the UK, which can offer high levels of care and support.

Commenting on her visit to a co-housing retirement scheme, television personality Joan Bakewell wrote: 'Who wants to be herded together with oldies in ring-fenced holding camps at the doors of death? No thanks. Who wants to be cut off from the laughter of children, managed by busybody managers in some British equivalent of America's condominium living or sunset cities? Again, no thanks.' However, plenty of people – and growing numbers of them – do want to be 'herded together' in this way.

Joan Bakewell wrote, in the *Guardian* on 3 June 2006, about yet another type of scheme, whereby older people were getting together of their own accord and setting up co-housing developments. Co-housing, she writes, is 'neither sheltered housing nor commune. It is a concept neatly balancing autonomy and support and it is entirely welcome.' Bakewell mentions one such enterprise, already up and running, Cold Street Farm in Dorset, where six like-minded people in their 50s and 60s bought an old farmhouse and a group of holiday cottages between them. They eat together twice a week yet they all have their own front door and privacy.

So – retirement housing is by no means all the same.

To take another, similar example, Caroline Sharman moved to a co-housing project in her 60s. She and five others clubbed together to buy a big house plus holiday cottages in Gillingham, Kent, and converted it into six separate units with communal facilities such as a laundry, guest suite, common rooms and shared meals in the main house.

Caroline moved into the house in November 2004, on her 67th birthday, and says it is like a new beginning. She says:

> It's great being with like-minded people. Before this I was looking after my old mum who lived to be 96.
>
> We didn't know each other that well when we bought the house together but we had many combined interests. In particular, we were interested in sustainable living. The communal rooms are in the main farmhouse and we hold courses in personal development and how to set up a co-housing project.
>
> We have two shared meals together a week and take it in turns to do the cooking, then we each give half a day to take care of the admin, cleaning, shopping, gardening and general maintenance. And we meditate together every morning! After that we have a brief chat about what's going on, and these times constitute the glue that keeps the project hanging together.

Caroline adds that 'personal issues' do arise, but a very strong bond has developed between the co-owners, and everybody wants what's best for each other. But she says it's not all hard work, by any means. 'We celebrate birthdays by going out for meals. There is always somebody to go out with, which is an advantage, and we can shop for each other and share cars. I definitely think that co-housing is the way forward for an ageing population, and we all need to be open to change and challenges.'

The six co-owners, four women and two men, were all in their 50s and 60s when they bought the property, and Caroline admits that they have not yet addressed all the issues of getting older, such as infirmity, dementia and lack of mobility. Caroline feels that the project gives her a sense of purpose and prevents her from slipping into grandma mode.

It's an idea that other homeowners, particularly those who are widowed or divorced and are now on their own, might like to copy.

Obviously, great care has to be taken with setting up the project from a legal and resale point of view. None of the co-owners in Caroline's set-up has resold, but such a scheme would have to be legally watertight in order to work. And you would have to be certain that everybody paid their way and contributed to their fair share of the maintenance and upkeep. Again, this is something that would have to be discussed carefully in advance, as nothing breaks up well-meaning projects faster than arguments over money.

If you do decide to move to sheltered or retirement housing, it is important to make sure the development is a member of the Association of Retirement Housing Managers (ARHM). This ensures standards are kept and that there is a grievance procedure in place should you have any complaints about the way your development is being managed. John Mills, Policy Officer, explains. 'We are committed to high standards in the management of private retirement and sheltered housing, and we have a management code approved by government. We manage around 95 per cent of retirement housing and are now moving into retirement villages, where housing and nursing care meet.'

But, whatever the pros and cons of sheltered housing, there are important financial decisions to make that will inevitably affect your eventual inheritance tax liability and disposable income in the meantime.

Most retirement apartments are sold on long leaseholds and you will not be the freehold owner. In most cases, the freeholder will also be the developer, such as McCarthy and Stone. Where there are bungalows or separate houses in a development, you may become the freehold owner, but you will still be required to pay service charges for management and maintenance. As a freeholder, though, you will own the property in perpetuity and are not subject to a running-down lease. The long lease usually runs way beyond your expected lifetime and is, at least when new, typically 99 or 125 years. The danger comes when the lease gets below 80 years, as after this the value of the unit will start to go down.

Management organizations are responsible for a wide range of duties, which include appointment of scheme managers, opening and operating bank accounts, garden maintenance, insurance, health and safety checks, organizing annual residents' meetings, preparing specifications and obtaining tenders for work, auditing accounts and recovering unpaid service charges. Not all of this work is easy to see, which makes some residents wonder what on earth they are paying all this money for, although the government does set limits for management fees chargeable on retirement housing.

There will usually be a reserve or sinking fund, as with other leasehold properties, but in any case you are governed by what it says in the lease. In general, retirement housing operates in much the same way as ordinary leasehold housing, except that in the retirement sector there are greater expenses, as many more services are provided.

If you are buying a retirement apartment in a new development, as opposed to a resale home, you will first have to reserve the flat of your choice and pay a deposit of around £250. This is not normally refundable should you change your mind.

You will then have to appoint an estate agent to sell your existing home and instruct a solicitor, who will check the contract and the lease. Supposing you have been successful in selling your home, you will exchange contracts and complete on this and then do the same with the retirement apartment. If you are rich enough, you might like to buy the retirement apartment before selling your previous home, although the vast majority of retirement home purchasers will have to sell their existing home first.

It may be possible to get a mortgage, if required. An interest-only or lifetime mortgage may be more suitable than an ordinary repayment mortgage, but obviously you will have to have enough income to pay the mortgage, service charges and council tax, as well as utilities and food.

If you are buying into a new scheme not yet completed, you need to know what will happen when the development is fully sold. The most important question to ask here is: what will happen to the freehold on completion of the development? A change of landlord may produce different charges. For instance, in one scheme there was initially free underground parking for residents. When the freehold changed hands, the new owner introduced a parking charge to which the car-owning residents understandably objected. They took the matter to the leasehold valuation tribunal, which ruled that the new owner had a perfect right to charge for parking.

In ordinary leasehold housing, there has been a concerted move in recent years to enfranchise, which is for the residents to buy the freehold collectively. Enfranchisement expert Kat Callo has this to say about retirement housing enfranchisement:

> Some retirement blocks qualify for collective enfranchisement while others do not. The determining factor is the identity of the landlord.
>
> If the landlord is a charitable housing trust and the housing is part of the trust's charitable functions, then the building does not qualify for CE [collective enfranchisement]. But commercially owned and developed retirement housing does qualify for enfranchisement, so long as all the usual requirements are met, which are: there should be at least two flats in the building, the flats must be self-contained with their own front door, and a minimum of two-thirds of all flats must be held by long leaseholders. A 'long lease' is usually defined as having 21 or more years left on it. Also, at least 50 per cent of the flats must take part in the enfranchisement to qualify.

The advantage of CE is that you now own a share of the freehold and can choose your own management company, or self-manage if you prefer. Working to bring about CE is a lot of hard work, can be expensive and is only worth it if you are deeply dissatisfied with the existing structure. You need a lot of energy and, also, it is a help to have time on your side, as CE can be a long-drawn-out process. For these reasons, it is very rare indeed for retirement complexes to enfranchise, although not completely unknown.

Sycamore Court, in Oxted, Surrey, collectively enfranchised in 2005, and manager Debbie Mayhew admits that they are 'very unusual' in this respect. She explains how it happened:

> We were built originally by Bovis, who sold on the freehold after completion. This is extremely common in the retirement home sector. In our case, this meant that we had a very remote landlord who didn't seem to care about the development, and residents felt they were not getting much for their money. A group of interested people got together and bought the freehold for ourselves. And it didn't even cost the residents anything!

How was this? Usually, when an apartment building collectively enfranchises, it has to pay a large sum of money to the freeholder to compensate for loss of income through service charges, ground rents and assigning new leases when old leases run out. Just working out the price is a highly complex business, and freeholders often challenge the figures, making the whole business expensive, fraught and long drawn out.

But – retirement homes have an X factor that does not apply to ordinary apartments, and that is the transfer premium of 1–3 per cent that has to be paid to the freeholder when a unit is sold. Debbie Mayhew continues:

> We worked out how much the transfer premiums, collectively, would come to, and managed to borrow a sum of money to buy the freehold. Now, every time a unit is sold, the transfer premium goes towards paying off the debt.
>
> We wanted a harmonious family place and we have now created this. Sycamore Court is now owned by the residents, each of whom hold one share in the company, and elect their own board of directors. The apartments are sold on long leases of 99 years, but effectively the freehold is shared amongst the owners, which means there is nobody making any money out of the development.

It is even more remarkable that Sycamore Court was able to enfranchise, as it is designated 'very sheltered housing', which means that it has 24-hour on-site staffing. There are a total of 23 staff members at the development, which gives it a very high staff-to-resident ratio. Debbie Mayhew says:

> But there were enough people here who wanted to do it, and now we are completely self-managing. We are now looking at the whole issue of the transfer premium, which is now in our hands. Previously, owners who sold on, or their executors, just had to pay it, and we felt we weren't seeing anything back for the money we were paying.

Other recent reforms regarding leasehold properties also apply to retirement housing, such as exercising the right to manage, buying a lease extension of 90 years if your lease is getting dangerously short, and the right to challenge service and maintenance charges at a leasehold valuation tribunal.

But you may not be allowed to sub-let if, say, you would like to rent out your home while you go on a round-the-world cruise for a year. Again, it is essential to understand all the terms and conditions, as retirement housing is often a law unto itself and is not the same animal as ordinary leasehold housing.

By far the great majority of older people living in retirement housing are single, but this is not always the case. If you are a married couple, or want to move in with a partner, you will have to think about how to organize the title deeds, so that the survivor will be able to remain in the property after one of you dies. All retirement housing has an age restriction, so if you have a partner very much younger than yourself you may be refused the purchase. Similarly, children are not allowed and pets are most likely not allowed, either, although some schemes do allow small, well-behaved pets.

Most retirement flats come unfurnished and, as the rooms tend to be smaller than those in the average house or flat, you may find that your existing furniture no longer fits. This means buying new furniture at a time when you may no longer be up to going round furniture shops. If this is the case, I suggest going online, or getting a techie grandchild or other relative to do it for you, and looking up Ikea and seeing what will fit into your new space. There are now a number of firms that deliver and assemble Ikea and other flat-pack furniture and, as it is both cheap and extremely well designed, it suits retirement flats very well indeed.

Although many people buy brand-new retirement housing and, indeed, there is a lot of competition to be the first in a new development, obviously resale, or second-hand, homes are coming on to the market all the time. Buying a resale retirement home is very similar to buying any property, but there are some important differences. In the first place, a resale home may well be cheaper than a brand new home, and you may want to think about this when deciding to buy a retirement home, as the value does not always increase over time.

It is now becoming more common for ordinary estate agents to handle retirement housing, and you will often see resales on the market with high street agents in the local paper. But it is still the case that many retirement housing companies have their own estate agents to deal with resales. Some retirement housing has restrictions – which will be detailed in the lease – on how homes can be resold. For instance, some leases will state that only those at or above the age limit can buy the property, which means the home cannot be bought on behalf of an older person by, say, their children. Some management organizations also have to approve a buyer, as is common in apartment blocks in the United States. This 'approval' is not a personality issue, but to make sure all buyers are of the right age group, are not too elderly and are in reasonably good health. If you are very infirm or disabled, you may not be able to buy into retirement housing and this means you should, ideally, buy into these schemes before you really need to, as by the time you actually need sheltered housing it may be too late.

Selling

As buyers of retirement housing are already fairly elderly, such homes often change hands. And, as when you buy, the management organization may have to approve the buyer. Because this type of housing cannot be bought and sold on the open market in quite the same way as other housing, often its value does not go up much. In addition, you – or your executors – may have to pay a premium back to the freeholder when you sell. The most common fees payable on selling are a fee for approval of assignments (when a lease changes hands this is known technically as 'assigning' the lease), a fee for approval of the purchaser by the management organization, and a contribution to the reserve fund. It is very common to have to pay this on reselling a retirement home.

The Age Concern book *Choices in Retirement Housing* makes the point that leases of retirement housing are well known for having assignment fees based on a percentage of the sale price, usually 1 per cent. It is not common – indeed I have never come across it – to have to pay to assign the lease for other types of leasehold property.

You will also commonly have to pay 1 per cent of the resale price back to the management company; this could go up to 2 per cent or even 2.5 per cent of the resale price on some leases. Another clause to watch out for is that the management company can end the lease if the owner becomes too old or infirm to be able to live independently.

Because retirement housing differs in many important ways from ordinary leasehold housing, it is in your interests to find out just what the lease says before buying. Although some clauses may be considered unfair or unenforceable, a lease is a legal document and you cannot pick and choose which clauses you will accept. Again, for buyers previously used to living in freehold houses, these leases with their many clauses and schedules can come as an almighty shock.

Note that some leases of retirement housing (although not in the ordinary leasehold sector) require the leases to be surrendered when the property is sold. This means you give up your lease, in return for a suitable sum of money of course, and the management company issues a new lease to the new owner. This means that the management organization controls the sale.

It is the case that older retirement housing tends to have far more restrictive leases than newer developments. As the sector has developed, the leases and conditions of purchase and sale have become much more user-friendly. It is also the case that buyers have become more canny and have demanded these changes. In addition, the sector has become extremely competitive, so developers have to offer better deals and conditions than they did originally.

Buying a lifetime lease

There is yet another option with retirement housing and that is to buy a lifetime lease. This is a relatively new idea whereby you can buy a lease that means you will have complete security of tenure and never have to pay any more rent. The only thing is, you do not own the property and it reverts to the landlord when you die.

This is another scheme devised by the enterprising Grainger Trust, and Peter Couch explains:

> Say you have a £200,000 house and you want to trade down to a retirement home. You can either buy the retirement home outright for £100,000 – or whatever the home costs – or you can buy a lifetime lease for, say, £50,000. This means that you will have a handy £150,000 in the bank, to spend, use on travel or give your children or grandchildren a leg-up on the property ladder.
>
> We have developed this scheme, which is going to grow, as it is such an attractive solution for, say, a 75-year-old who has a valuable home but not much in the way of savings. The other benefit is that the property does not have to be sold when the occupant dies. It can be quite tough selling retirement homes, especially for the executors, as they can only be sold to qualifying people and not on the open market.

How does buying a retirement home affect IHT?

In general terms, not at all. A retirement home, if bought on a lease or, in rare cases, freehold, still forms part of your estate when you die and is therefore subject to inheritance tax in the same way as any other asset. But as retirement housing is age-exclusive, and buyers have to be approved by the management, you would not be able to get around IHT by selling or giving the home to a relative.

With married couples or those in a registered civil partnership, the IHT exclusion still applies.

For some people, the renting solution, described in Chapter 4, may well be the answer, as you then retain your capital and do not have to bother about selling at a time when you may be too old or infirm to handle the sale effectively. As a nation, we have become fixated on buying, but it is not always a sensible option for older people, especially those who would like to dispose of some of their financial assets while they are still alive, rather than having them compulsorily seized by the Chancellor. IHT planning becomes much easier when you rent, rather than buy, a retirement home.

The 'middle way' solution of buying a lifetime lease, which comes halfway between renting and owning, gives security as well as enabling you to budget accurately and is definitely something to consider.

7 Buying a house with your adult children or for your elderly parents

Buying a house with your adult children

For some people, the prospect of living with their aged parents, or with their grown-up children, would be their idea of hell.

But – it is becoming ever more popular and there are some obvious advantages. You can, between you, probably buy a bigger and better house than you could otherwise afford, and there are other advantages in that you can help each other out if need be. In fact, this growing trend harks back to the Continental idea and also the old system whereby all members of one family lived together. This happened in the TV series *Dallas*, of course – but whether the idea is popular in the United States in real life is another matter. The large and growing number of retirement villages would suggest otherwise.

The classic sitcom *Sorry!* starred comic actor Ronnie Corbett as a middle-aged man still living at home with his mum. The humour, for us the viewers, lay in the sheer horrifying unthinkability of such a scenario.

Yet agents and property finders are noticing ever more of these extended family combos setting up home together and often buying grander and more expensive properties than they could afford as a single unit.

'The big attraction is you can get far more bricks and mortar by pooling resources in this way', says James Greenwood of Stacks Property Search and Acquisition, a company that finds suitable homes for clients, according to a blueprint. 'The idea began to bite in a big way in the early 2000s, in its modern format, and is becoming increasingly common. In a way, it harks back to the traditional Indian idea of the extended family.'

Many of us may feel we would rather live in the boot of a car or a dismal rented hovel than have to share a home, however grand, with *either* our elderly parents *or* our grown-up children. So why is this old-style, all-under-one-roof arrangement, with its echoes of the TV series *Dallas*, returning?

'So far as elderly parents are concerned, the big fear is that one's entire inheritance will be wiped out by nursing home fees', says Greenwood. 'Once a parent goes into a nursing home, the house value can be swallowed up immediately. The cost of nursing care facing every family with elderly parents is definitely one of the drivers behind this trend.' There is more on care homes in Chapter 8, but it should just be said here that if the family home is jointly owned then it cannot be taken away as it is no longer owned by the person going into a care home.

But there are other factors behind this seemingly strange trend. Unlike the previous generation, a lot of people coming up to middle age have never managed to get on to the property ladder themselves. So joining forces can also be a way of helping your middle-aged children get out of rented accommodation and into a nice home. In fact, figures from the Bank of England in March 2007 showed that the richest section of the population is now the 55–64 age group, who have benefited mightily by huge hikes in house prices since 1990.

'People also have ever less faith in the welfare state, and buying together can be the best way of caring for elderly parents and grandparents', adds James Greenwood.

> And when the arrangement works, it can be a wonderful way of increasing quality of life for all concerned. Grandparents and grand-children often get on extremely well, and there can be positive social benefit here. It's a way of bringing families back together again, rather than having all members scattered hundreds of miles away from each other. It is something increasingly to think about.

So how would it all work out? The inhabitants will most probably only want to see each other occasionally, and be able to live their separate lives, with facilities to have separate visitors. This means that there should, ideally, be separate bath rooms, a separate front door or access if possible, and maybe a separate garden. Certainly there should be a separate living room. However close you may imagine you are when living miles apart, living together can become extremely claustrophobic if you are too much on top of each other all the time and can never escape.

Before ever embarking on such an arrangement, it is a good idea to book a holiday together of, say, two weeks, where you are all living in the same villa, and see how much you get on each other's nerves. If you start to annoy each other when on holiday and in a temporary situation, how much more will you annoy each other when living together all the time? Many families come to grief over imagining they will all get on, simply because that is what families, in an ideal world, are supposed to do.

But most estate agents advise that, when separating out the facilities, you have to be sure that the home can easily be returned to its original layout, if necessary, as two completely separate units not only have adverse tax implications but also devalue a large family house. The house has to be able to return to its original layout without too much disruption.

'When it comes to finances', adds James Greenwood, 'we advise clients that they have to be very clear about who pays for what, and that it is essential to talk to accountants and lawyers before going ahead. You can never proceed on the basis that, because it's family, everything will be OK without a legally binding agreement.'

Tax adviser Paul Ffitch, of the company Sayers Butterworth, believes there can be many tax advantages to families pooling resources in this way, provided the arrangement is properly set up. 'If two families, or related adults, are moving in together as their main home, this means there is no capital gains tax on the sale, for either party. It can also be quite a nice way of inheritance tax planning, as the share will go to the survivor tax-free. This is a little-known escape clause in the IHT rules.'

The important aspect is that the shared home constitutes one residence, and has not been turned into two separate apartments.

'If you divide the home into separate residences, you then encounter problems', says Ffitch.

> In the first place, you will increase council tax liability and you will also fall foul of the IHT rules. The crucial point, when it comes to paying tax on the property, is whether you are living as one extended family or as two separate units. To avoid IHT on the death of one party, you would have to be able to prove that, although you own a share of the property, you have a right of access to the whole property.

Caution: Inheritance tax rules can be complicated here and it is advised that, before ever embarking on such an arrangement, you check very carefully to see what the IHT situation will be in your case, as individual circumstances can make a big difference.

In general terms, as we have seen, the only exemption for IHT is between spouses or partners, and Paul Ffitch's advice, which I have also seen elsewhere, appears to contradict the general situation whereby adult children, siblings or cohabiting partners can be turned out of a shared home on the death of one owner. It is very important, when setting up an arrangement of this type that you do not fall foul of the IHT rules or rules that say that a home can be sold to pay for nursing home fees.

There are now specialist companies offering inheritance tax planning, and it is imperative to seek advice from somebody conversant with all the ramifications before entering into such a scheme. When I asked an IHT expert about this, he said that it all depended on individual circumstances, and he could not give a definitive answer that would fit every case.

If you are an elderly parent, or an adult child considering buying jointly with an elderly parent, it is imperative to seek expert advice on *both* the IHT and the capital gains tax situation. The Revenue can take a very dim view of property arrangements designed to do the Treasury out of what it considers its rightful inheritance, and local authorities can also be draconian in investigating arrangements designed to avoid nursing home fees.

There can also be considerable dangers when one party – say the parents – puts more money into the purchase than the other. If you only want to be a half-owner, but you contribute, say, £500,000 to a property worth £600,000, you would have to live for another seven years for the purchase to become free of IHT, as before then you would be considered to have made a 'gift' of the IHT-bearing amount, which is £200,000 (in 2007).

Then, if your child moves out, the 'gift' amount would be treated as a 'gift with reservation' and, however long you lived in the house yourself, it would be included in your assets for IHT purposes. There could also be problems with your other children, who have not received any benefit from the shared house.

But it is not necessary for each party to contribute an equal amount of money, or even any money at all, for this arrangement to work in a legal sense. One party could stump up all the money, but the essential aspect is that both names must be on the title deeds, and there is a legal shared ownership of the property. 'You don't have to put a financial stake in to benefit', adds Ffitch, 'but both parties must be considered to own an equal share.'

But what if you realize, sadly, that with the best will in the world you can't live together after all and one of you, at least, has to get out. Can that person force a sale? Paul Ffitch advises: 'Where there is joint ownership, all owners have to agree, and it is not possible for one party to force a sale. This gives protection to both the ageing parent and the adult child.'

A lot of people nowadays, says Ffitch, are considering this type of arrangement instead of equity release, which is often the other option with elderly homeowners, as it keeps all the money within the family.

Case history

Sheila Ingham, 79, looks back on 10 happy years spent living in the same house as her son, daughter-in-law and their two children, now aged 13 and 10. Living together worked extremely well, she says, and the only reason it is coming to an end now is because her son and his wife are splitting up.

Sheila says:

It all started when my husband was very ill and my son and daughter-in-law suggested we bought a place together so they could help me look after him. I was delighted, but five months later he died. Their two children were then aged three and one. We lived together in the first house for two years and then eight years ago moved to this mill house in Woolaston, Forest of Dean. There are two acres of garden, which we have in common, but I had my own conservatory and courtyard, which was my private area.

Sheila believes it is vital to get all the finances arranged on a proper, legal footing before you start. 'It is essential to decide who pays for what and how council tax, for instance, should be divided up. It is also very important that you each have your own private space.'

The Mill House required a lot of work and, again, they contributed equally. 'We made sure we had our own separate areas but we had communicating doors upstairs and downstairs. This meant that I could babysit and go straight into their area, if necessary, but we were never on top of each other.'

Because of the marriage break-up, the house went on the market in 2006 at £539,950. Although it is being sold as a single unit, it has recently been viewed by a family looking to do exactly the same thing. 'It worked well for us', says Sheila, 'and I would recommend it so long as you can each have your own space.'

Sheila has now met a new partner, and they have bought a place together. She adds:

Because we sat down and worked out all the finances and percentage shares before we bought the place, now we are selling the property there are no arguments about who gets what. It is essential to do this; otherwise there can be terrible problems if the arrangement breaks down or ends for any reason. For us, the arrangement started smoothly and – at least in financial terms – it's ending smoothly as well.

Case history

A friend of mine, Peter, decided to join forces with his elderly mother when she became a widow, and together they bought a magnificent manor house in Surrey. When I went to visit I was suitably impressed and Peter said, 'This is what you can do when you put two ordinary houses together.'

Peter had a wife and two teenage children at the time of moving, and the arrangement worked extremely well, as his mother had her own separate quarters. The main problem that had to be addressed was how to make it fair to Peter's sister. So what they did here was to give the sister a sum of money from the sale of their mother's house, which would satisfy her and mean that the big house would not have to be sold on Peter's mother's death to administer the will. In the event, she lived for five years after they moved in together, by which time the teenage children had grown up and left home. Peter and his wife sold the big house not long after his mother died and, with the proceeds, bought a flat in Central London and a house in France, both mortgage-free.

There are two distinct ways of registering joint ownership of a property: joint tenancy and tenancy in common. With a joint tenancy, neither individual can sell without the other's agreement and, should one party die, then the survivor automatically inherits the other's share without the need for probate or adhering to the provisions of the will. The joint tenancy aspect will override these considerations.

Should you opt for tenancy in common, however, the situation becomes very different. This allows each owner to dispose of his or her share separately and, after one owner's death, that person's share passes into his or her estate. This may mean the survivor has to sell the property to pay inheritance tax.

Whatever you do, it is imperative that both names are on the title deeds. Otherwise, there is no ownership. If your name is not on the title deeds, it doesn't matter how much deposit you put down or whether you are paying the lion's share of the mortgage. Even if your name is on the mortgage agreement, it makes no difference if your name is not on the title deeds.

It is also essential to reflect your contribution by a declaration of trust, which is a legal document drawn up by a solicitor. It should go without saying that you should never, ever, ever trust anybody with very large sums of money or significant financial assets – even if they are your own children. If you have only one child, then there will be no problem so far as the other children are concerned with a joint purchase of this type. However, if you have more than one child, you have to consider carefully how the others might feel, especially if the one involved in the joint purchase is going to inherit a whole wonderful house when you die – and maybe leave the others without anything.

You need to be absolutely sure that your child or children have your best interests at heart – and sadly this is not always the case. Alexander Chancellor, writing in the *Guardian* on 23 February 2007, had this to say:

> The charity Action on Elder Abuse recently published a chilling report saying that middle-aged sons and daughters were the people most likely to rob their parents. It said that 53 per cent of theft, fraud and deception against elderly people was committed by their children. Millions of pounds of assets were involved. 'Often, the people who abuse older people are exploiting a special relationship,' says the charity on its website. 'They are in a position of trust, whether through family bonds, friendship or through a paid caring role.'

Chancellor goes on to say:

> It appears that children are the main culprits. How can they be so callous? Their parents are sitting ducks, of course. They tend to trust their children and can't imagine they would want to do them any harm. And as they get older, and their minds duller, they tend to defer to their children's judgments about whether they should hand over assets, sell their houses, give them power of attorney, or whatever.

This is wise advice and, if you are an elderly parent, you must make sure you are not bullied by your grown-up children into signing up to an arrangement that benefits them far more than it benefits you and that you do not really want. In very many ways, older people with property or other financial assets have become sitting ducks not only for the Treasury, local authorities and equity release advisers to relieve them of their hard-earned cash but also, sadly, their own children. The charity Action on Elder Abuse believes that there is far more abuse of the elderly by their own children than by carers in nursing homes or hospitals – even though this is the kind of abuse one frequently reads about.

Older people can become very frightened of their own children, particularly when those children may be better educated, more professional and more literate and moneywise than the parent. This may be particularly the case with an elderly widowed mother who may not have ever handled money on her own account and now leans heavily on the advice of her son who works in a bank (say) and who seems very confident of what he is saying. Never, ever sign any document you do not fully understand.

But supposing you are in full agreement, how does it all play out, tax- and moneywise?

Those who have done it say that it is essential not only to have totally separate living quarters but to separate the finances as well, remembering that this is, above all, the type of purchase where you are joint owners, not where one party buys the house for the other to live in. I would say it is essential to draw up a document, lodged with a solicitor, that states how bills such as council tax, utilities, repairs, cleaning services, gardening or other costs will be met.

The easiest way of doing this is to set up a joint account to which each owner contributes the same amount, and then set up direct debits for all the expenses that you have agreed form part of the shared living arrangements. Normally you would not have to have two separate television licences and there would be one council tax bill, as well.

It is all too common, when dealing with your own family, not to bother about legal arrangements or proper documentation, on the grounds that you 'trust' each other. But if, say, you move in with your son and his wife and they later divorce, the wife may want to get her hands on quite a lot of the shared equity. It is vital to take this possibility into account, however remote it seems at the time.

Of course not every eventuality can be covered by a piece of paper, but any documentation should clearly state the situation at the time and what will happen in the event of a sale taking place, a death or other later consequence, and for all those named on the title deeds to sign the document in front of a solicitor. Informal arrangements only lead to chaos, tragedy and recriminations later.

I cannot emphasize too strongly the importance of legally witnessed paperwork, *especially* when dealing with family members.

As regards the ever-present subject of inheritance tax, this will eventually have to be paid by somebody after death. Jointly owned houses, being bigger than ordinary properties, will almost certainly go above the IHT threshold.

Buying a house for your elderly parents

If you have elderly parents who have been renting and have only their state pension plus any benefits to live on, you may wonder whether it is worth investing in a house or flat for them, which you will sell on their death.

This is again quite a popular arrangement for children who have done well themselves, to give their parents a comfortable home for the rest of their lives as well as, with any luck, providing themselves with a property investment that will increase in value. If you and your siblings get on together, you could join forces to do this.

In the 1960s, it used to be common for rock stars from working-class backgrounds to buy their parents a bungalow once they had made it big themselves. In fact, buying your parents a bungalow became a rock star cliché for a time. It still happens, although it no longer makes news. Most rock stars offload at least some of their fortune to buy their parents a nice home, and it can also prove to be a good investment for those who are comfortably off but not necessarily on rock star incomes.

You would probably not be able to buy a designated retirement or sheltered home for your parents, so you would have to look for somewhere on the ordinary market. Depending on your circumstances, you could buy somewhere either outright or on a buy-to-let mortgage, and you would have to work figures out very carefully to make sure that the investment was a wise one. In other words, you would need to make sure that the purchase plus the rent your parents would pay (if any) would give you an operating profit plus capital growth.

Don't forget that here we are talking about buying a place for parents who have never been able to afford a place of their own and who have been paying rent all their lives. Although there may not be many of these left nowadays, as 85 per cent of the over-60s now own their own homes, they do still exist.

There is another small class of elderly people who have lost their once-owned houses on divorce or separation or who have perhaps had bad business reverses. We all know of once rich and famous people who have ended their days in rented accommodation, living on benefits. The film director Roy Boulting ended his days on benefits, in a rented flat, and I have a friend in this position, a former magazine editor who held down many big jobs in her time but who now lives in a housing association apartment near Hove, Sussex, and has absolutely no money at all. Such a person would be a prime candidate to have a property bought for her by a son or daughter.

My late friend Judy Cousins was also in this position. Judy was born Lewen Tugwell and registered a sex change in the 1970s. On divorce, Judy gave her ex-wife the house and had no money left over to buy somewhere else. She rented a two-bedroom council flat, and in the 1980s came the opportunity to buy it. Judy, who had become a sculptor by now (one of her more famous pieces was a bronze head of Denis Thatcher), still had no capital to buy the property, but it was a complete bargain. In the event, Judy's son-in-law bought it and Judy continued to live in it, now paying the son-in-law rent, rather than the council. Judy lived in the flat for another eight years before she died and the by now very valuable property went to her daughter and son-in-law. Under the right-to-buy scheme, the flat was initially sold at a bargain price, but by the time Judy died the property, situated near the famous Ascot race course, could be sold at the proper market value. Usually, if you buy a property from the council under the right-to-buy scheme, you have to already be living in it and then continue to live in it for another four years before the property can be sold on.

Buying a property for your elderly parent(s) could also be a way of giving them security for the rest of their lives. Elderly people without any money or property of their own can be extremely vulnerable, and buying them a home can be a way of making both of you comfortable – you because you have a valuable investment and the parents because they now have a nice secure home.

So far as inheritance tax, capital gains tax, income tax and all the other taxes go, this arrangement can be very simple.

You, either singly or together with your siblings, put up an amount of money to buy the property. You will usually be able to get an 80 or 85 per cent mortgage, so you will have to put up some capital. You then ensure that the names of all those buying into the property – legally up to four people can buy property together – are on the title deeds. The parent moving into the property would then pay you rent so that you could afford to keep up mortgage repayments. If the parent is on benefits, the local authority would have to come and assess the place, to see whether the allowed benefits would cover the rent. People on housing benefit usually get their council tax paid as well, and this would also have to be determined, along with any other benefits to which they might be entitled.

Renting a home from your children would not necessarily invalidate benefits, but again everything has to be researched before deciding to buy a property. Local authorities all allow certain levels of housing benefit, but these differ and, in any case, are subject to regular alterations by the authority concerned. In most cases, benefits advisers check up regularly on benefit recipients.

When the parent dies or has to go into a nursing home, the property will revert to you in exactly the same way as with any other tenant. This means you can either rent it out to somebody else or sell it and pocket the proceeds.

Inheritance tax here would not apply, as you have simply invested in a property that you happen to have rented out to your elderly parent. You would most likely have to pay capital gains tax on the sale of the property but, with any luck, you would have received rent all those years and also the property would have increased in value to give you an overall profit when you came to sell.

But if your parent can be considered an elderly dependant, you may escape the capital gains tax rules.

My late partner, John Sandilands, bought a house for his then 83-year-old mother to live in, imagining that she would not, at that age, live for very much longer. In the event, she lived for another 10 years, by which time the house had increased mightily in value. John sold the house at a good profit and, with the proceeds, became a buy-to-let investor himself. Because she was an elderly dependant, John did not have to pay capital gains tax on the profit.

This is again something worth investigating, as capital gains tax rules can be complicated. Although it took John a decade to realize the profit on the house, it was very welcome indeed when he was eventually able to sell it. So – buying a property for your elderly parent could also be a neat way of financing your own old age. If I had an elderly poverty-stricken parent who did not own his or her own property, I would be very tempted to do something like this.

But, in order to make it work, you would have to treat it in exactly the same way as any other investment and make sure everything is documented and drawn up with a solicitor. Often, parents and children can imagine that because they are close, or 'family', they can bypass legal arrangements. This is a terrible mistake and should not be entertained for one single minute. There should never be any loose ends, anything left to chance, and whatever the arrangement initially agreed this must be ratified in writing and a copy lodged with your solicitor.

8 Going into a care home

As medical care improves and life expectancy increases, ever more people are going to end their days in a care home.

In the past, there were, for the vast majority, few financial considerations at stake when this time was reached. My grandmother and great-aunt both ended their days in a care home and the state paid. There was no other way of funding such care, as my elderly relatives had no money or assets of their own, and both had lived in rented accommodation all their lives.

Nowadays, things are very different. The present generation of elderly and very elderly people are the first such generation in history to be sitting on considerable financial assets. Mostly, they own their own homes, which have probably been mortgage-free for many years, and even if they don't have much capital in the bank they at least have a fully owned valuable house worth well into six figures.

All such assets can be forcibly taken off them when they go into a care home, thus completely wiping out any inheritance they may have hoped to leave to their families.

So far, we have been talking mainly about the implications of inheritance tax, now affecting large numbers of older people for the very first time. But we come on to another financial problem facing older homeowners, which is that if you have assets over about £20,000, including your home, these may well be taken off you – compulsorily – to pay care home fees. So if you live long enough, or become too frail and ill to look after yourself, it could well be that care home fees will eat away at your inheritance long before the Revenue does.

In 2007, the average cost of a care home is £600 a week or £30,000 a year. This means that somebody with a home or other assets worth £300,000 will have their entire estate wiped out in a decade, should they live that long. And it is no longer so unusual for old people to last for 10 years or more in a care home. When the octogenarian father of a friend went into a care home, his daughter said: 'There's enough money to last for six years; then he's just got to die.' Luckily for the finances, he did die within the appointed time.

My former mother-in-law lasted just two months in a care home, whereas my own mother lingered on for 10 years. As with all aspects of getting older, there is no knowing in advance how long somebody will live once they go into residential care.

The whole subject of care home fees is a highly complicated area, and the Alzheimer's Society warns that the situation is far from transparent or easy to understand. But just to describe the basic situation, if you or an elderly relative is assessed as needing continuing NHS care you do not have to pay any of the costs of medical or nursing care. But if you have financial assets over the limit, you will still have to pay some costs, such as for meals, your room and incidentals.

Just to make matters even more complicated, there are two distinct types of care homes: nursing homes and residential homes. Nursing homes provide nursing care, but residential homes are aimed at people who do not need actual nursing but who can no longer look after themselves. Such people will most likely have to pay the entire cost of their care, unless their financial assets are below the limit.

In order to be eligible for continuing NHS care, whatever your financial situation, you must be diagnosed with a complex medical condition that requires specialized nursing support. However, definitions of this can vary from one area to another.

You should be assessed for continuing NHS care *before* going into a nursing home. If you are not awarded fully funded NHS care, this means that for some reason you, or your relative, have not met the criteria for needing specialized nursing care. People in residential homes have not normally been assessed for continuing NHS care and in most cases will not be eligible for an NHS contribution.

Then there are three different levels of NHS contribution, depending on the severity of your condition: high, middle and low.

Before you are admitted to a nursing home, as distinct from a residential home, you will be means-tested for all costs apart from nursing care. If entering a residential home, you will be means-tested for all care costs including any nursing care.

Supposing you have assets or savings of under £20,550, you will qualify for some help with bills. But if your total assets, including your home, go over the £21,000 mark, you will have to pay for your own care until this money runs out. If you own your own home, your assets will definitely be far in excess of the very low limit over which you can be asked to pay.

The big problem comes with the definition of what is meant by 'nursing care'. Although very few elderly people would probably choose of their own volition to go into a care home, not all are deemed to need the kind of medical care that qualifies them for full NHS support. The decision as to whether nursing care or 'social care' is required is taken by local primary healthcare trusts, many of which follow different rules. Age Concern estimates that around 75,000 people are having to pay their own care home bills when they should actually qualify for free care under the NHS.

A report in the *Daily Mail* on 27 February 2007 called this the ultimate 'postcode lottery'. Depending on where you live, you may be fully funded in a care home, whatever your financial assets. But in other parts of the country you will have to pay out of your own funds, with exactly the same level of disability.

In its ongoing 'Dignity for the Elderly' campaign, the *Daily Mail* has highlighted the difficulties the sick and old experience in securing NHS assistance, and has accused the government of raiding the savings and homes of older people in order to fund the black hole in the NHS.

The likelihood is that if you or an elderly relative has to go into a care home – and remember, abandon hope all ye who enter here as you will most likely never come out – the chances are that your entire life savings, including the home, will be wiped out long before you die. My mother, for instance, was admitted to an expensive care home when suffering from Alzheimer's. She was not expected to last long, but in the event lasted 10 years, with the result that there was nothing whatever in her estate when she finally died. Her decade in a nursing home had used up every bit and more of her money, which came mainly from the sale of her house, at around £200,000.

Many homeowners, anticipating some such scenario, wonder whether there is anything they can do to protect their assets in the event of having to go into a care home. The following letter to a newspaper is typical: 'I am a 67-year-old widow in good health, with no savings, just my pension. Should I put the deeds of my home in the names of my two children or put their names alongside mine, so the ownership is split three ways? I want to avoid paying if I need long-term care.'

The reply?

> If you have to go into a care home, your local authority might argue you had made over part of your house to avoid paying care home fees. This is known as deliberate deprivation. If proved, the local authority could still assess your home as though it all belonged to you and use its entire value to determine your fee contribution.
>
> There are other risks to consider. First, if you make your children co-owners of the house, they can do what they like with their portions.
>
> What's more, if either of them were to divorce, their share of your house could be included in any divorce settlement, which could have consequences for you continuing to live there. Second, there are no inheritance tax benefits. As you will live in the house, the share in it is a gift with reservation, so will never be exempt from IHT.
>
> Third, if your children already own their own homes in addition to their stake in yours, any future sale of your house could generate a capital gains tax liability for them.

Here is another typical case: a 90-year-old woman has to go into a nursing home. She has been assessed as being in the middle band of care needs, which means the NHS will contribute £83 a week to her care. The actual cost of her care is £600 a week. She owns a flat worth £150,000 and has savings of £5,000. What happens?

The situation here is that her flat would have to be sold and her savings used up to pay for the care. The value of her flat can be disregarded for 12 weeks, after which she will be expected to

pay the full cost of her care apart from the £83 a week contribution. Another problem is that if the money from the sale of the
flat is invested at, say, 5.5 per cent this will tip her into the
income tax bracket.

Apart from any other consideration, going into care, for those
who have savings or assets, is a financial minefield. In the case
above, it would be possible to buy an annuity, which is paid
directly to the nursing home to cover fees. A purchase price of
£71,000 would guarantee £2,250 a month. But nobody knows how
long a 90-year-old may live. It could be another 13 or 14 years.

The Nursing Homes Fees Agency (NHFA) also offers an
investment bond whereby, with a property worth £150,000, £45,000 is
kept back to pay for immediate fees and the rest is invested in a bond
to provide tax-free and penalty-free withdrawals when required.

If you, or an elderly relative, have to go into a care home and
have considerable assets, it would be worth contacting the
NHFA to see what they can offer. The other solution is just to let
the money run down until the elderly person dies, or there is
just no more in the kitty to pay fees, at which stage the NHS will
have to chip in.

The fact is that, if you do own property, there is no easy way of
avoiding care home fees, should you need long-term care in later
life. A BBC *Panorama* programme in 2005 highlighted the problems
many pensioners were now facing. The presenter, Vivian White,
reported that 40,000 homes are being sold every year to fund so-
called 'social care' in nursing homes when it actually legally qualifies as 'nursing care'. Nursing care is supposed to be free to all
under the NHS and yet many sick, elderly people are having their
homes forcibly sold from under them to pay for their care in
nursing homes.

When Tony Blair was in opposition in 1997, he said that he did
not want children brought up in a country where the only way
pensioners could get long-term care was by selling their homes.
When he had been prime minister for 10 years, nothing had
changed in this regard, although there was a case in 2006 where a
man had recovered £50,000 from the sale of his mother's house
when she had to go into care. He argued that her care was
'nursing' and not 'social' – and won his case, the first of its kind.

In this case, Mike Pearce's mother, Ruby, who died in November 2004, had spent the last six years of her life in a nursing home suffering from Alzheimer's. Although his mother obviously needed full-time care, her NHS trust in Torbay assessed her as being in the middle band of nursing care and therefore eligible for £70 a week help. As her nursing home fees came to £1,250 a month, the only choice was to use her savings and sell her home to meet these costs.

The problem, put in its simplest terms, comes down to this: those who have saved all their lives to buy their own homes have to pay fees, while those who have made no provision at all for their old age have their fees paid. Just over 25,000 people have their fees paid in England and Wales.

As we saw earlier, it is the definition of what constitutes 'nursing care' that is at the heart of the problem. Age Concern commented: 'We are not talking about people who have difficulty walking up the stairs, but those who are doubly incontinent, are effectively bedridden and completely confused. Despite this, many are still not assessed as needing 24-hour care.'

On the *Panorama* programme, the government's position was defended by health minister Liam Byrne, who reiterated the stock argument that application of the rules about social care versus nursing care was the responsibility of individual healthcare trusts. In any case, he added, people no longer had to sell their homes immediately to fund their care, as trusts could now postpone claiming their costs until after the patient had died.

If you are considered to need 'social care' rather than 'nursing care' and you have financial assets, these will be taken away from you until you have nothing left, and there is no real way of disposing of your assets before such care is needed and giving them away. Even if you have given them away, social services can demand them back. In its way, the fear of having to pay huge care home fees at the end of life is as great as the inheritance tax fear.

The vast majority of older people go into care homes when they can no longer look after themselves and when they are quite beyond being looked after by a spouse or relative, however loving or devoted. Very few older people go into care homes before this stage is reached. It is possible, in some cases, to arrange a home care package, but this will be expensive as well. One very old lady I know has round-the-clock nursing care in her own home – at a cost of £100,000 a year. This has already been going on for several years, and luckily she is rich, but these costs are still eating away at her estate, however considerable.

As we have seen before, it is no longer legally possible to make yourself destitute by disposing of all your assets while you are alive. You have to be able to show you are able to live at the same standard as before you gave away the assets, although of course any substantial financial gift made more than seven years previously will not be called back to pay for a care home or care package.

If somebody is assessed as needing care in a care home, the first thing to happen is that social services will carry out a detailed financial assessment to decide how much the person will have to contribute to the cost of their care. This includes both income and capital, for instance income from investments, buy-to-let or interest on capital at the bank.

If the home is not sold within a certain length of time, the local authority can put a legal charge on it and claim back what is owed when the house is sold. If the home does not sell quickly, you may be eligible for an interest-free loan to cover the cost of care home fees until the property is sold.

But if the home is also occupied by a husband, wife, unmarried or civil partner or close relative under the age of 60, the value of the home will not be taken into account. This is where it can be advantageous to buy a house jointly with a member of your family. However, husbands, wives and civil partners may be asked to make a contribution as 'liable relatives', as there is a legal principle that husbands and wives have a duty to maintain each other. No other relative can be considered 'liable' in this manner.

In the case of a husband and wife where one partner has to go into care, the local authority has no right to assess a spouse's finances, and can only ask for a contribution they can afford. If no agreement can be reached, however, the local authority may go through the courts to settle a 'reasonable amount'.

Here is another very typical situation. A married couple are in their early 80s and the husband, who has severe Parkinson's, now has to go into a care home. His own home, worth about £250,000, is in his sole name, not in joint names. He has always been the chief breadwinner and, although the home cannot be taken to pay for the care home, his pension and any other income can be seized as a contribution to care costs. This leaves his wife unable to manage. What happens here?

Caroline Bielanska, chair of Solicitors for the Elderly, says:

> Most older people these days are asset-rich, cash-poor, and problems intensify when one half of a couple has to go into a care home. We deal with masses of cases where people are not funded by the NHS for their care and often there is no easy answer. In the case above, the husband's income will be used to pay care home fees, which may leave his wife very near the poverty level. If the wife sells the home and moves somewhere smaller, the cash released will then be used to pay care home fees until there is nothing left. So that is not the answer, either, apart from which it is very difficult to suddenly uproot when you are in your 80s.
>
> If such a case came to us, we would first of all look at all the ways in which the wife would be able to survive when her husband's income is being used to pay care home fees. There will be an automatic reduction in council tax, and then there may be benefits and allowances she can now claim. We would investigate all of these and also ask at what point the state would pick up the tab.
>
> Our advice is to make sure you see a specialist lawyer before anybody has to go into a care home, to work out your best financial options. In another case, the husband had to go into a care home and the wife was left in a 400-year-old cottage which badly needed repairs which she could not afford. If she sold the house, any spare money would then immediately be used to pay her husband's care home fees, yet she could not stay in the house as it was. Our solution here was to advise her to take out some equity release to pay for the repairs so that she would be able to continue to live in the home.
>
> As the house was in the husband's sole name and he had lost capacity, we had to apply to the court of protection to get the equity release. If she had sold the house, any liquid assets left over would go straight into the kitty to pay the fees.

Legal advice is also needed, adds Caroline Bielanska, as some care homes charge a placement fee of around £3,000, which is non-refundable.

> To us this is not good practice so we would urge potential patients or their carers never to sign a care home agreement without having it carefully checked first, as it could constitute an unfair contract. The Office of Fair Trading have been looking into such contracts, as few people approaching the need for a care home have much energy or expertise to look carefully at contracts, engage solicitors or research their rights.

Where one party has been diagnosed with dementia, the best thing is to contact the experts, the Alzheimer's Society, who have much excellent advice to offer on the subject of paying for care home fees and assessing the level of care needed. In many cases, say the Alzheimer's Society, sufferers are assessed as needing social, rather than nursing care, as dementia is not always seen as a bona fide medical condition.

But the Alzheimer's Society is very much a campaigning charity and, as they are working hard to get dementia recognized as a serious old age illness needing nursing care, the more grist they have to their mill the better.

Power of attorney

It is sensible, when you are getting older, to appoint somebody totally trustworthy as your attorney. This means he or she has power to act on your behalf should you later become incapable, confused or vulnerable. Briefly, there are two distinct types of power of attorney: ordinary power of attorney and lasting power of attorney (called enduring power of attorney before April 2007).

There are a number of ways, informal and formal, that you can appoint somebody else to deal with your affairs, and it is probably safe to say that the more money or assets you have the more careful you need to be. Elder abuse is extremely common, especially among those who have large financial assets. Solicitors for the Elderly say they have many cases on their books where neighbours do shopping for elderly neighbours and then help themselves to the spare change. 'But,' says Caroline Bielanska, 'if that neighbour does not help out, the elderly neighbour cannot get her shopping in, so what is the answer?'

I myself do regular shopping for an elderly couple, who have plenty of money, and I always make sure I get a receipt for everything I buy for them. I also ask them to write a list and I tick every item off once I have bought it. But not all neighbours, or relatives, are so honest, and elderly people with cash assets are ripe for abuse.

If you are living on your own and finding it difficult to get to a bank, building society or post office, you can set up a joint account with a trusted friend or relative, which gives that person authority to draw money on your behalf. Or you could set up a third-party mandate, whereby a friend or relative can access your account but is not given a card or your PIN.

But if you give somebody power of attorney, this means that to all intents and purposes that person becomes *you*, and can sign cheques, take out money, pay your bills and – if not totally honest – take your money without you necessarily knowing anything about it. There is much legislation in place to prevent abuses but, even so, they are widespread. Parents commonly give their children power of attorney, usually when they are becoming frail. Very often, parents want to believe their children are perfectly honest and trustworthy but in many cases they are not. It is very common for an adult child who, say, lives near you and visits frequently to suggest power of attorney and talk it up, so that you have signed before you really know what you are doing. Then you have lost control of your own financial affairs.

The best time to set up a power of attorney is long before you need it and to have more than one attorney. This prevents – or at least cuts down the likelihood – of one attorney raiding bank accounts.

With a simple power of attorney, the friend or relative can access your account but, strictly speaking, has no entitlement to funds. You as the donor decide which powers the attorney is to have, and an ordinary power of attorney only lasts so long as you are mentally capable of making decisions. You can if you like authorize your attorney to sell your house on your behalf.

If you wish somebody to act for you should you become mentally incapable, you need to set up a lasting power of attorney (LPA). Although this must be signed while you are still capable of understanding what you are signing – and I know from experience that capacity tests vary a lot – the LPA has far wider powers than the ordinary power of attorney. To all intents and purposes, the attorney is now you and can act in every way as if he or she was you, including making far-reaching decisions for you about healthcare and care homes. The attorney will, for instance, be able to do anything with your property that you may have done yourself, including selling it. This authority will continue if you become mentally incapable.

When considering giving power of attorney to other people, you should ask yourself whether those you are considering handle their own money well, whether they have ever been in debt or had a county court judgment against them and whether they have enough money of their own not to be tempted by your bank accounts or assets.

Parents, especially elderly parents, are notorious for giving a black-sheep-type offspring yet another chance. Children can be extremely manipulative, jealous, dishonest and grasping, as a thousand novels and court cases show. Such cases are less rare than might be imagined.

Although the attorney is legally liable if the money is not handled in a proper capacity, it is up to the rest of the family to challenge this. And if there is no money left, as is often the case, there may not be much point. There is also the important aspect of asking yourself whether appointing a particular person as your attorney will cause rifts or disagreements within the family.

While you are capable of making your own decisions, you are allowed to make them even if they seem eccentric or unwise to others. For instance, if you wanted all your money to go to an animal charity and were perfectly compos mentis, nobody would be allowed to override that decision. It is only if you have lost mental capacity that such decisions may have to be made for you.

Those who have lost mental capacity are at great risk of financial abuse and, although it can be argued that if you have lost capacity it may not much matter to you what happens to your money, other beneficiaries or heirs might be concerned.

It should be said that, although there are powers in place to prevent abuse of power of attorney, it is probably impossible to track down every such case. Attorneys have a lot of power, especially where there is a considerable estate, and you need to be 100 per cent certain, before ever they are appointed, that they will always have your best interests at heart. The only way of determining this is to go on past behaviour – not on wishful thinking for the future.

Attorneys cannot draw up wills on behalf of the donor, and the will remains sacrosanct. Manipulative children or family members can, however, prevail upon an elderly, confused and vulnerable person to change his or her will in their favour and, again, courts are littered with such cases.

All powers of attorney in any case end on death, and the will then comes into its own. This means that inheritance tax is unaffected by power of attorney, unless, of course, the attorney has successfully emptied all the accounts, sold any property and then fled the country. And this happens far more often than people might imagine.

Powers of attorney must be properly witnessed by a third party and, although you can get forms from any law stationers or online, I would always advise consulting a solicitor who specializes in dealing with the affairs of older people. Solicitors for the Elderly specialize in such matters as consent capacity and decision making, financial planning for retirement and long-term care, wills, probate and trust, lasting powers of attorney, tax planning, equity release plans and lifetime giving.

The best advice here is to see a solicitor who understands the needs of older people long before you have lost any capacity or need to go into a care home, and set up the power of attorney while you fully understand all the ramifications of this very significant document. Come to the decision on your own, and do not, as many older people do, allow yourself to be persuaded to sign a power of attorney by one of your children. This is the most usual way it works in practice, but it is far better if you do it unaided by somebody whispering in your ear.

The most common way that powers of attorney are set up is for one of the children to suggest it and, before you know where you are, a solicitor is round at the house with all the papers and you have been bludgeoned into it. Any other children or family members may not know anything about it. Solicitors, after all, are people working for money, not charity workers, and those who are not specialized in dealing with the needs of elderly people might not appreciate the bullying that may have resulted in the power of attorney being granted.

Receivership

If elderly relatives have not made a lasting or enduring power of attorney and become mentally incapable of handling their own affairs, it may be necessary to appoint a receiver to deal with their affairs. This has to be done through the court of protection (it cannot be an informal arrangement). A close relative, friend, bank manager or even the local authority can be appointed to act as a receiver. If no suitable person can be found, the court of protection can appoint a solicitor as receiver. Responsibilities are demanding and time-consuming, and a relative must decide whether he or she wants this extra work. Solicitors and banks, of course, charge for acting as receivers.

The job of a receiver is to manage income to ensure day-to-day needs are met and bills are paid, that any property is kept in a good state, that income tax is paid and that important documents are kept safe. The court of protection must authorize any use of capital on behalf of the person with dementia, and the receiver must liaise with the court about investments, sales and other financial matters.

The receiver has to submit annual accounts to the court of protection and take out a security bond to protect the assets of the patient. There are fees for all court of protection work although, when assets have come down to £12,500 or less, fees are reduced.

If you have elderly parents who are living in a house that is no longer suitable for their needs, or require a level of healthcare they are not receiving, how much should you interfere? This is a difficult one as, unless a power of attorney is given, you as their child have absolutely no jurisdiction over them at all, however strangely you feel they may be acting. In this situation, I would again go and see a solicitor conversant with the needs of older people and ask advice. It is also a good idea to contact the Alzheimer's Society and Action on Elder Abuse, as these charities are the experts and frequently deal with such cases.

Caroline Bielanska, of Solicitors for the Elderly, says:

> A major issue we deal with is bullying by adult children, especially when there are considerable assets at stake. Many very elderly people have not had much experience of lawyers, and they are afraid of costs and even of seeing a solicitor. We were set up especially to address the specific needs of older people and have guidelines on how to deal with bullying and abuse by members of your family. It is often assumed families are all totally wonderful and only want the best for their elderly parents, but this is often far from being the case. Very often, elderly people don't feel able to challenge bullying by their adult children and, although we hear a lot about how badly old people are treated in care homes, the sad fact is that most elder abuse comes from spouses or children.
>
> Since the 1970s, large numbers of older people have valuable assets such as property or shares and there is the temptation for the children to say: that's my inheritance. But it's not – necessarily.
>
> Very often, an elderly person will go to see a solicitor on the instigation of an adult child, who wants to be with them during the consultation. But we have to be clear about who exactly is our client and, if a 60-year-old son, say, brings his 83-year-old mother in to see us, we will not allow the son on the consultation. We have to be very sure that no undue influence is being put on the elderly person when it comes to changing their will, granting power of attorney, going into a care home, or selling their house, for instance.
>
> A good lawyer will always see the client alone and ask pertinent questions about other members of the family. For example, if an

elderly person wants to cut a family member out of the will – a very common scenario – we will ask why this is the case. We will then ask whether this will cause a serious family rift and, if so, do they care about it?

We are always on red alert when we suspect an elderly person has been leaned on by a member of their family, especially if that person is a named beneficiary.

It is also important to make sure your will is fair and will not alienate other members of the family. When the will of Lord Lambton, who died in 2006 aged 83, was published, it was found that he had left his entire estate, including his home in Italy, to his son and heir, Ned. His five daughters, including the television personality Lucinda Lambton, got nothing. Lucinda was philosophical about it in a newspaper interview, but such a will harks back to the old days of primogeniture, when the eldest son – or in this case the only son – automatically inherited everything.

In the old days, it was common for anybody who had anything to leave to bequeath far more to sons than to daughters, and even today all too many people do not even consider whether the will they are writing is perfectly fair to all beneficiaries. Not that a will has to be fair, of course, but it leaves fonder memories of you if it is.

Wills that attempt to control events beyond the grave should also be discouraged. A specialist will writer or solicitor expert in the needs of older people will help you to write a will that is as fair as possible.

A note on using banks, solicitors or other professionals to help with the financial needs of a very elderly person: if you are in the position of having to look after the financial affairs of a very elderly person who has become incapable of handling his or her own situation, you have to weigh up the work of doing it yourself against using a bank or solicitor. The latter option can soon become very expensive indeed. Solicitors charge around £200 an hour – some much more but few much less – and this very quickly adds up into thousands. Every half-hour spent on the telephone, for instance, or in a consultation, puts another £100 plus VAT on to the bill.

Banks are also notorious for charging extremely high fees for acting as receivers or executors. It is all a matter of how competent you feel you are to deal with situations that can become extremely complicated, both financially and in respect of how much time they take up.

The above information underlines how very important it is for elderly homeowning parents, older people who may be sitting on considerable financial assets, and also their adult children to think and research very carefully all the best options that may be available to them when it comes to care home fees, setting up powers of attorney, writing wills and naming beneficiaries and executors.

There are all too many people lying in wait and ready to relieve older people of all their savings, both professionals and family members. And to add to the difficulties, the great majority of very elderly people now in their 80s and 90s are not as financially astute as younger people, and simply do not suspect that either their own children or smart people in suits who come round to the house with gracious smiles and complicated forms to sign may just be trying to get at their money.

It is not easy and perhaps not even possible to avoid paying care home fees when you possess considerable financial assets. The main problem is that very few people ever research the care home situation until they are on the point of needing such care. My mother-in-law's family, for instance, only started their research into care homes when the old lady was about to be turned out of a state convalescent home and was not able to go back into her sheltered home. Thus, they had just a few weeks to research the care home situation before she had to go into one.

The best time to do research on care homes is long before you, or your elderly relative, actually need to go into one. I would say, start the research at least a year before the care home is needed; otherwise, you are at the mercy of social services and care home owners and may not have time to work out the best solution.

In fact, I would go one further. If you, or your relative, are aged 80 and still living in your own home, I would start researching care homes *now*. In the past, there has been enormous reluctance to face up to the fact that old people may not be able to go on living in their homes indefinitely. Older people have also themselves been extremely reluctant to make proper wills, to face up to appointing an attorney and to think about provision for their own care in their final years.

All too often, older people just exist from day to day, never making any satisfactory arrangements.

Conclusion

By now, the main message of this book should be clear: if you are an older homeowner, you will have very many options to choose from, all of which have their pros and cons. Setting aside for the moment any considerations about inheritance tax and the grim possibility of having to pay hundreds of thousands of pounds in care home fees towards the end of your life, which lifestyle options come out best?

Of course, your decision will be influenced not just by how much money you have, but by your circumstances, preferences and – most importantly – state of health. A person in rude health will most probably be making quite different decisions from those affected by Parkinson's, arthritis or another condition related to getting older.

My own solution, which has worked well for me, was to sell the 'big house' – not that it was all that big really, but it was a valuable house in an expensive part of London, and was also expensive to maintain. Also, I was living in a street full of families with young children, and the environment started to feel wrong. I decided to downsize to a more modest flat, which has a mixed community of young single people, older married couples, one or two young families and older single people – in fact more or less the full range – and I have not regretted it once.

My flat, on the first floor, feels safer than the house, where odd people were always knocking on the door, and it is also warmer and cheaper. The other fact, now that I live alone, is that there is companionship in an apartment building that might not be matched by living in a street of separate houses. The occupants of the building where I now live are not necessarily great friends, but we are neighbourly and often pop into each other's flats for a cup of coffee, drink or chat or have an evening in a nearby bar. Such companionship is not always easy to achieve in a road of separate houses. Another factor is that we can look out for each other, and this can become increasingly important as you get older. When living alone in my house, I could have been lying there dead for weeks before anybody would have thought to make enquiries. But in the apartment building, where there is a caretaker who has a key, this is unlikely to happen. I do some shopping for an elderly couple on the top floor who can no longer get out on their own. Again, this would not be so easy to arrange if you lived in a house.

Taking this option of downsizing to a much cheaper flat has given me a lot of money in the bank – money that would otherwise be tied up in bricks and mortar and unavailable to me. I would also have the expense of maintaining a house and it would all be down to me, whereas in the apartment building we employ a firm of managing agents who are responsible for arranging maintenance.

It seems to me that nowadays it is most sensible for younger people with families to live in houses and for older, single people to live in flats.

When you are young and have at least potential earning power, having cash at the bank may not be that important. But it becomes more necessary as you either head towards retirement or your earning power starts to decrease. Very many older people these days are retiring with far less money in their pensions than they expected to have, and this situation is not likely to improve with time. Final salary-based pensions are on their way out and more or less the only people who can rely on a reasonably comfortable pension are those working in the public sector – civil servants, teachers and local government workers. We are told to save for our retirement, but it is not always easy to save money out of income, and nor are most jobs as safe as they used to be.

For many, then, maximizing property assets during the earning years and then selling up to fund retirement will be the only real way of having enough money to last a lifetime without having to depend on benefits. Downsizing is the best thing to do, to my mind, if you will have enough money left over to make the effort worthwhile. There is little point in selling a £200,000 house to buy a flat for £180,000 – at least, not from a financial point of view, as there will be virtually no money left over from the move.

What about retiring to another country? Many of my friends have now done it, and not one has regretted the decision, although recently there has been a spate of television programmes about couples who excitedly retired to Spain, became ill and could not then afford to move back to the UK. Good health is not something that can be guaranteed at any age, but I don't think I would move abroad if I had a serious pre-existing health condition. Retiring abroad is only for those who are in good health – at least at the time of the move.

It can be exhilarating to up sticks in later life and move to another country, but you have to be very sure you would not be homesick and that you would enjoy living in that country permanently. When the late Liz Tilberis moved to New York to edit *Harper's Bazaar*, she and her husband, Andrew, sought out a special 'British store' that sold such un-American delicacies as toad-in-the-hole, Welsh rarebit, black pudding and marmalade – items they had not eaten for years, or perhaps ever, in the UK. Homesickness, she reflected in her book *No Time to Die*, can take many strange forms, and you do not always know what you will miss until it's not there.

But many older people have discovered that moving to another country gives them a renewed zest for life, and a feeling of embarking on a wonderful adventure. Some say very boldly that there's not a thing they miss about the home country. Mostly, though, you cannot expect that your children will want to take over the foreign home. Broadcaster and writer Dr Mike Smith and his wife, Nonie, now in their 70s, are selling their French home. They say that their three adult children and grandchildren love to visit the place but are not interested either in maintenance or in paying the bills. They just want the free holiday. So – a foreign home will not necessarily provide a welcome legacy.

The other possible option, renting in later life, can also, I believe, be a very sensible decision, and this is bound to grow as renting starts to become chic again. Getting out of property ownership when you are older can also give you a very nice lump sum in the bank. This option also provides a valid alternative to commercial equity release. As yet, renting is not something that has occurred to many older people, but I believe the idea will soon take hold and become extremely popular, as it has so much to recommend it. But in order for renting to work for the older market, there does need to be security of tenure. Assured shorthold tenancies mostly last only for six months at a time and they are in any case geared mainly towards young professionals who are always on the move.

What about retirement housing? I think that really depends on individual preferences, as feelings about sheltered homes are so hotly divided. Some people feel they would hate to live in a compound with just other elderly and infirm people, while others appreciate the comfort, security and serenity that this type of housing can provide.

It is also worth noting that the kind of home you may turn up your nose at when you are a very active 60 can seem a wonderful prospect when you are a less mobile 80 – by which time it may be too late to be considered for a sheltered home.

The attractive idea of getting together with some of your friends and buying a large house between you, which you then divide up into apartments, can work, but needs a lot of careful thought, as you have to know in advance what will happen when one of you dies or has to go into a nursing home. I like the idea of living in a big house with my friends – so long as we could be completely separate of course – but the practicalities can be hard to work out. But so far, I have not had the confidence to pursue this idea. Then you have to ask yourself: would you want your close friends to be that close all the time? Perhaps it is a good idea to keep some distance.

The worst thing you can do, to my mind, is to stay in the family house long after the family has gone and long after the house meets your current needs. This is the case especially if you can no longer afford repairs and, even if you could afford them, you don't have the energy any more to embark on extensive renovation.

All too many older people, as *Guardian* writer Patrick Collinson said, are living in houses that are too big for them and desperately in need of repair. But you can't just tip the occupants out; many older people feel extremely resentful about being expected to downsize just because they don't use all their bedrooms. And, as Mark Rees pointed out, how do other people know what's too big or too small for you?

What is clear, however, is that if you are going to make a move you should do it before you actually need to, because once you can no longer manage the stairs or drive a car to the shops it may be too late to be able to exercise a free choice in the matter. It is a good idea to move to a smaller house or a flat when you still have the energy to declutter and look for somewhere else. Although many older people are understandably reluctant to move, they are usually glad when they have made the effort, as they find their new home is so much more suitable for them.

You may love gardening, but for how long will you be capable of handling a large garden? My in-laws constantly moved to homes with large gardens, huge gardens in fact for the size of the house, then towards the end of his life my father-in-law admitted that he had never really been a keen gardener. Considering the vast gardens he had always had, this was a real revelation – and it had taken him 75 years to face the fact. His final home before he died was an upstairs flat in a very small age-exclusive development where the garden was taken care of by the maintenance staff. He loved it!

Taking wise property and lifestyle decisions in later life requires a lot of hard, straight, sensible thinking, bearing in mind that mobility, finances and enthusiasm may all decline and change as you get older. Also, attitudes may change. A few years ago I did a lot of DIY. Now I have run out of energy and, instead of spending weekends up on ladders painting ceilings, employ contractors to do the work for me. Nobody wants to be old before their time but it pays to anticipate your possible future needs.

Commercial equity release can be a good idea, if there is really no other way of giving yourself enough money for your retirement. But do bear in mind that the value of your estate will be severely diminished as a result and that you will effectively put yourself in hock to a financial institution for the rest of your life. However, if you need a large lump sum *now*, and are determined not to move, equity release can be a good way of getting your hands on it.

Whatever you decide to do, it is imperative to sit down and talk about all the possible options with your partner or your family and make sure you are all in agreement as to the best solution for you. At the same time, it must be *your* decision, reached entirely alone.

It is sensible for married couples and civil partners to make mirror wills, but if you are likely to go over the inheritance tax threshold consult a solicitor about making mirror wills and ask about nil-rate discretionary trusts.

If you have children or grandchildren to whom you would like to leave money or assets, also discuss these with an independent financial adviser or solicitor conversant with IHT regulations (not all are equally expert, by any means) to make sure you decide on the best course of action for you. In my case, when making my latest will, I felt my grandchildren were too young to be considered. Every few years, though, I will look at my will and revise it if circumstances change. The very worst thing you can do, now that IHT is a very real possibility for large sections of the population, is to have an out-of-date will and one that no longer reflects the current situation.

Whenever you move house or have a new grandchild or your own children's circumstances change, you should update your will. You will also need to make a new will should you meet a new partner in later life or lose a former partner through death or separation. These days, circumstances can change very frequently, and wills must always reflect the current situation to be of any use.

You must also always make a new will if you decide to retire or move abroad permanently, as UK wills may not be valid in the chosen country. Ask about this before moving.

It is rarely possible to avoid IHT altogether if you have assets above the nil-rate band, but it can be delayed or minimized by careful will writing. Also make sure your will is scrupulously fair to all parties. The Society of Will Writers (yes, there is such an organization) say that families split apart by unfair wills never ever recover. Wills are dramatic and important documents, and need a lot of care and attention to get right. If you own property, do not put off writing your will.

It is extremely common for families to fall out when there is money around. This has always been the case and no doubt always will be the case. When families squabble over wills or inheritance, they usually say it's not the money – but it always, always, is. Where there is no inheritance to worry about, there is no disagreement.

The sad fact is that a lot of older people have housing decisions forced on them, by bullying children, by salespeople touting equity release or by increasing age and infirmity. And nowadays ever more people are having to take on board inheritance tax and possible nursing home fees when thinking about what to do for the best in later life. The taxes and costs that have to be considered in later life are inheritance tax, capital gains tax and nursing home fees. If you are not careful, you can find yourself clobbered by a triple tax whammy. You, or your estate, will pay inheritance tax when you die, and you will also be liable for capital gains tax and nursing home fees while you are alive.

Capital gains tax, just to remind you, is levied on the sale of any asset that makes a profit, apart from your principal private residence. These assets can include paintings, antiques, and stocks and shares, as well as property, including any foreign property.

With money and property come complications, so I hope this book will give all older homeowners the confidence to make their own decisions, with their own best interests in mind. You, the homeowner and the owner of the financial assets, must come first.

Resources

General

The Retirement Show (held in London in July, covering all aspects of retirement living, including sheltered homes, renting, living abroad and equity release), www.The-Retirement-Show.com

Chapter 1: Inheritance tax

Books:

Lowe, Jonquil (2005) *The Which Guide to Giving and Inheriting*, 8th edn, Which?, London

Scott, Maria (2006) *How to Avoid the Inheritance Tax Trap*, Daily Telegraph Books/Robinson, London

Advice on setting up discretionary trust wills:

http://www.tenminutewill.co.uk
http://www.taxationweb.co.uk

Solicitors specializing in IHT planning:

Sayer Moore Solicitors
Tel: (020) 8945 0323
www.sayermoore.co.uk

The Max Gold Partnership
www.maxgold.com

Advice on probate:

www.theprobateadvisoryservice.co.uk

The Pensions Advisory Service
www.pensionsadvisoryservice.org.uk

www.inheritance-tax-online.co.uk

http://www.whathouse.co.uk/mortgages/inheritance-tax

ISB Independent Financial Advisors (specialists in IHT planning)
Tel: (01732) 471629

The Society of Will Writers and Estate Planning Practitioners
Eagle House
Exchange Road
Lincoln LN6 3JZ
Tel: (01522) 687888
www.step.org

HM Revenue and Customs: useful leaflets:

IHT2 Inheritance tax – Lifetime gifts
IHT3 Inheritance tax – An introduction
IHT5 Inheritance tax – How to calculate the liability
IHT8 Inheritance tax – Alterations to an inheritance following death
IHT18 Inheritance tax – Foreign aspects

Chapter 2: Staying put

Advice on care and repair:

http://www.careandrepair-england.org.uk/sisosig/prog/html

Elderly Accommodation Counsel
3rd Floor
89 Albert Embankment
London SE1 7PT
Advice line: (020) 7820 1343
e-mail: info@eac.org.uk

HOOP: Housing Options for Older People
http://hoop.eac.org.uk/hoop/about-hoop.aspx

'Lodging a belated protest', John Sandilands on lodgers
www.johnsandilands.info

Guides to equity release:

The Help the Aged Equity Release Service
St Leonards House
Mill Street
Eynsham
Oxford OX29 4JX
Tel: (01865) 733009
e-mail: equityrelease@helptheaged.org.uk
www.helptheaged.org.uk/equityrelease

NatWest
Tel (for information on equity release): 0845 877 6000

Prudential
Tel (for free information pack on equity release): 0800 234 6925
www.pru.co.uk/info

Home reversion specialists:

Bridgewater (part of the Grainger Trust)
www.bridgewaterequityrelease.co.uk

In Retirement Services
http://www.inretirementservices.co.uk/why

Daily Mail Guide to Unlocking the Cash from Your Home by Charlotte
Beugge
Tel (for free guide): 0800 915 3131

Key Retirement Solutions
Freepost NWW201A
Preston PR2 2ZY

Independent Equity Release Advice
Tel: 08080 555 500
http://www.agepartnership.co.uk

The Equity Release Information Centre
Tel: 0800 298 6288
http://www.askeric.org.uk

Norwich Union
Tel (for lifetime mortgages): 0800 404 6220
http://www.norwichunion.com/lifetime-mortgage/index.htm

unbiased.co.uk (independent advisers)

Chapter 3: Downsizing

Book:

Sangster, Chris and Gillean (2004) *The Downshifter's Guide to Relocation*, How To Books, Oxford

Property Price Advice (accurate house pricing)
www.propertypriceadvice.co.uk
Tel: Louisa Fletcher, 07771 993 901

Property search company:

www.bdiproperty.com

Estate agent websites:

www.findaproperty.com
www.rightsearch.co.uk

Chapter 4: Renting instead of buying

Book:

Hodgkinson, Liz (2006) *The Complete Guide to Letting Property*, 6th edn, Kogan Page, London

Retirement renting companies:

Girlings Retirement Options
Tel: 0845 758 356
www.girlings.co.uk

The Grainger Trust
Citygate
St James Boulevard
Newcastle-upon-Tyne NE1 4JE
Tel: (0191) 261 1819
e-mail: info@graingerplc.co.uk
www.graingertrust.co.uk

Affordable rented retirement flats and bungalows:

Anchor Retirement Housing
www.anchorhousing.org.uk

Selling your house and renting it back:

Fullhouse Developments Ltd
Tel: 0800 234 6586

Chapter 5: Moving and retiring abroad

Books:

Hobbs, Guy (2006) *Retiring to Spain*, Vacation Work, Oxford
Knorr, Rosanne (2001) *The Grown-Up's Guide to Retiring Abroad*, Ten Speed Press, Berkeley, CA

Government guides:

http://www.directgov.uk/BritonsLivingAbroad

Foreign and Commonwealth Office (retiring overseas: essential information)
www.fco.gov.uk

Leaflets:

IH121 Income tax and pensioners
GL29 Going abroad and social security benefits
SA29 Your social security insurance, benefits and healthcare rights in the European Economic Area

Department for Work and Pensions
The Pension Service, International Pension Centre
Telephone Liaison Unit
Tyneview Park
Newcastle-upon-Tyne NE98 1BA
Tel: (0191) 218 7777
www.thepensionservice.gov.uk

Electoral Commission
Trevelyan House
Great Peter Street
London SW1P 2HW
Tel: (020) 7271 0500
e-mail: info@electoralcommission.org.uk
www.electoralcommission.org.uk

Retirement Pension Forecasting Team
Department for Work and Pensions
Newcastle-upon-Tyne NE98 1BA
Tel: 0845 3000 168
www.dwp.gov.uk

National Insurance Contributions Office
Centre for Non-Residents
Longbenton
Newcastle-upon-Tyne NE98 1BA
Tel: 0845 300 168
www.dwp.gov.uk

Age Concern Information Line
Freepost (SWB 30375)
Ashburton
Devon TQ13 7ZZ
Tel: 0800 009 966
www.ageconcern.org.uk

The Association of Retired and Persons Over 50
Greencoat House
Francis Street
London SW1P 1DZ
Tel: (020) 7828 7132
e-mail: infor@arp.org.uk
www.arp.org.uk

Help the Aged Senior Line
207–221 Pentonville Road
London N1 9UZ
Tel: 0808 800 6565
www.helptheaged.org.uk

Consular Directorate
Foreign and Commonwealth Office
Old Admiralty Building
The Mall
London SW1A 2PA
Tel: (020) 7008 0218
www.fco.gov.uk

General information on emigration:

http://www.migrationmatters.com/retirement.php

Elderly Accommodation Counsel (housing care in Europe)
http://www.housingcare.org/search/elderly-housing-abroad.aspx

International banking:

Barclays
Tel: 0845 601 5901
www.internationalbanking.barclays.com

Retirement villages abroad:

The Villages, Orlando, Florida
www.thevillages.com

Australia (information)
www.retirement-villages.com.au

Chapter 6: Sheltered and retirement housing

Books:

Age Concern (2006) *Choices in Retirement Housing: Your guide to all the options*, Age Concern, London

Callo, Kat (2006) *The Survivor's Guide to Buying a Freehold*, Lawpack, London

Hulley, Annie (2006) *Spending the Kids' Inheritance*, How To Books, Oxford

Useful websites and addresses:

Advice, Information and Mediation Service (advice service for people living in retirement housing)
Astral House
1268 London Road
London SW16 4ER
Tel: 0845 600 2001
e-mail: aims@ace.org.uk

Centre for Sheltered Housing Studies (training organization)
1st Floor
Elgar House
Shrub Hill Road
Worcester WR4 9EE
Tel: (01905) 21155
www.cshs.co.uk

The Leasehold Advisory Service (LEASE) (advice on leasehold matters)
2nd Floor
31 Worship Street
London EC2A 2DY
Tel: 0845 345 1993
e-mail: info@lease-advice.org
www.lease-advice.org

Retirement Care Marketing (agent for resales)
43–45 High Road
Bushey Heath
Herts WD23 1EE
Tel: (020) 8901 0300
www.rcg.com

Retirement Homesearch
Freepost BH 1044
New Milton BH25 5ZZ
Tel: 0845 800 5560
e-mail: enquiries@retirementhomesearch.co.uk
www.retirementhomesearch.co.uk

Churchill Retirement Living
Tel: 0800 783 7661
www.churchillretirement.co.uk

McCarthy and Stone
www.mccarthyandstone.co.uk

The Grainger Trust (buying a lifetime lease)
Citygate
St James Boulevard
Newcastle-upon-Tyne NE1 4JE
Tel: (0191) 261 1819
e-mail: info@graingerplc.co.uk
www.graingertrust.co.uk

Retirement Villages
Tel (information): (01372) 731888

Retirement Villages UK
Tel: 0845 607 6405
www.Richmond-Villages.com

www.SeniorOutlook.com

Publication:

Karen Croucher, *Making the Case for Retirement Villages*, Joseph Rowntree Housing Trust, York Publishing Services Ltd, York
Tel: (01904) 430 0033

Advice on buying the freehold:

Rosetta Consulting
e-mail: info@rosettaconsulting.com
www.rosettaconsulting.com

Management company:

Guardian Management Services
www.guardian.org.uk

Association of Retirement Housing Managers (ARHM)
Southbank House
Black Prince Road
London SE1 7SJ
Tel: (020) 7463 0660
e-mail: enquiries@arhm.org

Economic Lifestyle (equity release for retirement homes)
6/7 Lovers Walk
Brighton
East Sussex BN1 6AH
Tel: 0800 043 3365
e-mail: info@economiclifestyle.co.uk
www.economiclifestyle.co.uk

Very sheltered housing:

Sycamore Court
Hoskins Road
Oxted
Surrey RH8 9QJ
Tel: (01883) 723500
www.sycamorecourt.co.uk

Sunrise Senior Living
Tel: 0800 652 8484
www.sunrise-care.co.uk

Retirement Security Ltd
Tel: (01789) 292952
e-mail: mail@retirementsecurity.co.uk

Chapter 7: Buying a house with your adult children or for your elderly parents

Book:

Hanson, Michele (2006) *Living with Mother Right to the Very End*, Virago, London

Chapter 8: Going into a care home

Publication:

When Does the NHS Pay for Care?, produced by the Alzheimer's Society and supported by Age Concern, Help the Aged and the Royal College of Nursing (guide to fully funded nursing care)

Available from:

The Alzheimer's Society
Dementia Care and Research
Gordon House
10 Greencoat Place
London SW1P IPH
Tel: (020) 7306 0606
Helpline: 0845 300 0336
e-mail: info@alzheimers.org.uk; helpline@alzheimers.org.uk
www.alzheimers.org.uk

Age Concern
Tel (information line): 0800 009 966

Counsel and Care (information and advice on care homes)
16 Bonny Street
London NW1 9PG
Tel (advice line): 0845 300 7585
e-mail (advice): advice@counselandcare.org.uk
www.counselandcare.org.uk

Relatives and Residents Association (advice for relatives and friends
of people in care homes)
5 Tavistock Place
London SW1H 9SN
Tel (advice line): (020) 7916 6055
www.relres.org.uk

Carers UK
20/25 Glasshouse Yard
London EC1A 4JT
Tel (carers line). 0808 808 7777
e-mail: info@ukcarers.org
www.carersonline.org.uk
Booklet: 'Residential and nursing home care'

Care Standards
National Care Standards Commission
St Nicholas Building
St Nicholas Street
Newcastle-upon-Tyne NE1 1NB
Tel: (0191) 233 3556
e-mail: query@ncsc.gsi.gov.uk
www.carestandards.org.uk

Solicitors for the Elderly

To find a specialist solicitor, contact:

Julie Cameron
Room 17
Conbar House
Mead Lane
Hertford
Herts SG13 7AP
Tel: (01992) 471568
e-mail: jcameron@solicitorsfortheelderly.com
www.solicitorsfortheelderly.com

Index

Index of Advertisers